How to

Receive

greater

Anointing

How to

Receive

greater

Anointing

DAVID RAMIAH

Christ Exalted Ministries
~Transforming Lives To Transform Their World~

Christ Exalted Ministries

"MY heart is inditing a good matter: I speak of the things which I have made touching the king: my tongue *is* the pen of a ready writer." Psalm 45:1

If you would like further information, please contact us here:
Christ Exalted Ministries
21197 – 3975 Jane Street,
Toronto, Ontario, Canada, M3N 2K0
www.ChristExaltedMinistries.com

How to Receive greater Anointing
Copyright © 2010 by David Ramiah. All rights reserved.

This book is designed to provide accurate and authoritative information with regard to the subject matter covered. This information is given with the understanding that neither the author nor Christ Exalted Ministries is engaged in rendering legal, professional advice. Since the details of your situation are fact dependent, you should additionally seek the services of a competent professional.

Book design copyright © 2010 by Christ Exalted Ministries.
All rights reserved.
Cover design Ainsley Samms
Editing Mrs. Joy Hallwood

Published in Canada
ISBN: 978-0-9733247-7-8
Printed in the USA
2nd Printing 07.11.11;
1st Printing 03.03.10

ACKNOWLEDGMENTS

Father God, thank you for the privilege and honour of writing this book. To be able to hear your voice for your children, and to be able to receive from your heart what you desire to share with them, is the most wonderful thing to me. Yours is the glory and the honour and the power. Amen.

To all the members of Christ Exalted Ministries: thank you for allowing me to be me; to present to you God's word as He gives it to me and to minister to you in the way I do. May God bless us all, and cause us to grow up in Him in greater measure and to a higher degree always.

Special thanks to Mrs. Joy Hallwood for her many hours spent editing this book. God bless you, Joy!

Many thanks to my Mom and Dad who always stand by my side, no matter what, and to the rest of our family who believe in me and in what I do. I love all of you, including my brand new niece, Isabella.

CONTENTS

Introduction

It was February of 2003 and I was on a mission's trip in the Amazon of Brazil. I was on the missionary boat, "Zany Silva." I was with a Dentist, a Doctor, the crew, and other missionaries from The Central Presbyterian Church of Manaus. The Zany Silva carries medical and dental supplies, to the natives living along the banks of the Amazon River. After a five day journey we were on our way back to the City. It was Saturday.

I was relaxing in a hammock. I was reading. Soon, I began to doze off. I decided to retire to the cabin for a snooze. This was in the middle of the afternoon, about two thirty. Slipping away into my cabin, I slept soundly and had a dream.

In this dream I saw a man of God preaching in a big auditorium of some sort. I was seated in the front row to his left and I was watching him closely. Suddenly, he stopped. He turned and looked straight at me. With his left hand he pointed his index finger directly at me and proclaimed, *"There is a greater anointing coming!"*

I told no one who that man was until after September 16th 2008. Even though I told people about the dream and preached for three weeks in my church on "greater anointing;" and though I wrote a booklet at that time called "Greater Anointing," I told no one who that Preacher was. I believe that I may have been waiting for my dream to come through first.

It was Tuesday night, September 16th 2008. It had been a long day and I was resting on the couch. Turning on the television I switched from one channel to another. Really, I wasn't looking for anything in particular. But, as I kept changing the channels, I came across Benny Hinn on CTS - channel nine in Toronto. And having no interest in watching anything really, I switched to another channel. Immediately, I heard the Lord speak into my spirit, "Go back and listen to what He has to say."

What do you think Benny Hinn was preaching on? You are absolutely correct if you thought that he was preaching on "anointing!"

The more he preached on the anointing the more I knew what he was going to say. Suddenly, with such passion, greater than I have ever seen in him, he proclaimed to the audience, "I am going to prophesy! I am going to prophesy!" He paused. And suddenly he screamed out, "There is a greater anointing coming!!"

Where did I hear that before!?

I was so overjoyed to see Benny Hinn on television with my own my eyes; and to hear him with my own ears prophesy word for word, in the very fashion that the Lord gave it to me almost six years prior.

My friends, the hour has come, the day is today, and the time is now. What I understood from this dream is that this Greater Anointing is coming to prepare the Body of Christ for the Rapture. Be ready to receive greater anointing from the Lord! The Lord said that He is sending it, and so it will be. Be wise in this hour. Heed the call. Make the crooked ways straight. Strengthen the feeble knees. Lift up the hands that hang down. Get ready! Hallelujah.

"And whosoever shall exalt himself shall be abased; and he that shall humble himself shall be exalted." Matthew 23: 12

Do not be high minded in this hour. Do not be wise in your own eyes. Humble yourself and you will be exalted. Many are called, but few are chosen. Live your life as if Jesus Christ might come today to take His Body - the Church, to be with Him. Watch and pray as the Bible says. You never know when the Lord will come. But in the meantime, be ready! Greater anointing is coming.

"SURRENDER YOUR ALL TO HIM AND YOU WILL RECEIVE ALL OF HIM."

Chapter One

Greater Anointing

Is there such a thing?

> "....the angel of the Lord appeared unto him in a flame of fire out of the midst of a bush: And he looked, and behold, the bush burned with fire, and the bush was not consumed. And Moses said, 'I will now turn aside, and see this great sight, why the bush is not burnt.'
>
> And when the Lord saw that he turned aside to see, God called unto him out of the midst of the bush and said, 'Moses, Moses.' And he said,

'Here am I.'

And he said, 'Draw not nigh hither: Put off thy shoes from off thy feet, for the place whereon thou standest is holy ground.' Moreover he said, 'I am the God of Abraham, the God of Isaac, and the God of Jacob.' And Moses hid his face; for he was afraid to look upon God."

Exodus 3:2-6

There were no crackling sounds; no popping or scorching; perhaps not even a sound of flames blown by the wind.

The flock huddled together to one side. There was fear in their eyes. But they stayed in one place; wide eyed, they gazed at the sight. They seem to be kept in a bunch by invisible wings.

Suddenly at the corner of his eyes he saw a fire.

As Moses looked closely, he saw that the bush was still green and lush; it still there. Yet there was a fire all over it! But, it was not burning up. It was not a destructive fire.

He drew near to get an even closer look.

"Moses."

Shocked and frightened, he must have jumped back with his rod raised high in the air. He was ready to strike. He was prepared to defend himself from any attack. Obviously he wanted to know where the voice came from. Who was it? Who was calling out to him? Was there someone behind him? Was there someone around the corner? Perhaps the owner of the voice was behind another bush? Who spoke?

"Moses."

"Here am I."

"Take your shoes off. You are on holy ground."

Not only did he take his shoes off, but Moses must have bowed his head closer to the ground than he ever did before.

Whoever could set a bush on fire without having it burn up and disintegrate was no other than God. No other than God would know his name in this deserted Mountain.

He realised that he was in communication with the most awesome being in the entire universe. This was God! One snap of His fingers and Moses would be dead. One word from the Lord and it would all be over.

However, this was not about death and dying. It was not about getting Moses back on the throne that he had lost; Moses was at one time a son in Pharaoh's Palace. It was not about making him rich and famous. Neither was it to make him a greater shepherd. It was about calling and anointing!

God told Moses that He wanted him to go back to Egypt. But, he was not to return to live in Pharaoh's palace. It was to deliver Pharaoh's slaves.

> "And it came to pass in process of time, that the king of Egypt died; and the children of Israel sighed by reason of the bondage, and they cried, and their cry came up unto God by reason of the bondage."
> Exodus 2:23

Moses grew up in Pharaoh's house. He knew how powerful Pharaoh was. He understood the power that the man possessed. He was taught by the wisest in the Palace, and was trained by the greatest warriors in Egypt.

He knew the size of Pharaoh's army. He realised that it would have grown greater in number, and while he had been in the desert for the last forty years, it would have become mightier. He recognised that it would take the greatest army on earth to defeat Pharaoh.

But, Pharaoh's was the greatest army in the world! Who could defeat him?

No one was able to defeat Egypt for many years. They were a towering force. The Egyptians were a most mighty and dominant enemy to have. Who could stand in the face of Pharaoh and defy him? And who had power enough to take away the most treasured possession of this great nation? Who could take away from the Egyptians the ones who physically built most of what they had?

They were not going to let go of their most precious of treasures - Hebrew slaves.

So then, why is God asking Moses of all people to deliver His beloved Israelites? Why does He want to send this man back to Egypt?

"Go unto Pharaoh, and say unto him, 'Thus saith the Lord, let my people go, that they may serve me.'"

Exodus 8:1

Forty years of Desert

There was a time when Moses thought like an Egyptian, had the mindset of one of them, spoke like them, and lived as the people of Egypt lived.

As a king's kid; he wore the most excellent of clothes, rode in the finest chariots, had the most dependable and handpicked servants, slept in the most luxurious beds and ate the best food. For forty years, that was his life.

If God was going to use him though, he had to change.

Into the desert he was driven.

Another forty years went by before Moses heard the voice of God. With a grand unbelievable spectacle of a burning bush, the Lord got his attention. After many years had passed, God called out to him. He gave Moses a mandate, "Go and set my people free."

I assure you, it was not easy for Moses to hear this. Every fear in him of Pharaoh and of Pharaoh's wrath must have climbed up inside of him and grabbed him by the throat. Choking with fear, he pleaded with the Lord to send someone else.

However, God would not choose someone else. This is the man He had groomed for the job. This is the one He had saved eighty years prior; from all the children who died upon Pharaoh's command.

He was not going to call someone else. He had placed in Moses exactly what he needed to get the job done. And so, it wasn't going to take any amount of pleading or begging to change God's mind.

"Okay, you want an interpreter? One is on his way. He will be your mouthpiece. But, know this, you are going to get the job done!"

You have to understand that when God Almighty calls someone for a certain thing, He will not change His mind. The Lord will make sure that that person has the wherewithal to accomplish the task: Anointing, wisdom, understanding, gifts and talents, money, people, and everything that they would need to fulfill their call.

"For the gifts and calling of God are without repentance." Romans 11:29

However, God would not choose someone else.

Moses wanted to know how he was going to be able to do this thing that Jehovah - I am that I am - wanted done. God asked him, "What do you have in your hand?"

What you need to fulfill your call in life, is already in your hands.

For forty years, it was with a rod in Moses' hand that God groomed him. Instead of a king's sword or a slave-master's whip, he was taught and trained with a shepherd's staff in his hand. He learned to lead and protect simple, dirty and smelly sheep. He grew into a nurturer and caregiver, and in patience and in humility.

> *What you need to fulfill your call in life, is already in your hands.*

The Israelite's were not a highly educated or sophisticated people at all, in this time of their existence. They were for the most part simple slaves, following the orders of their taskmasters. All they understood was the whip on their backs and the yelling commands of their masters. They obeyed, and if not they suffered the consequences. But, they knew their God! And *they needed a leader who would be gentle enough, but trustworthy to lead them.*

After forty years in the desert, Moses was a totally different man. He had changed. He was a

more patient and tolerant person. He was not like the younger, quicker-to-act-than-think-it-through person. He was able to think things through more thoroughly now. He asked questions first, and acted later. He was better at working out problems and at negotiating with others than he was before. This Moses was an entirely different person than the one who came out of Egypt.

He had patience to wait on people who would be eager to act right away and not wait. They were enslaved for about four hundred years. They would not be willing to delay another day to get out of Egypt! Would you blame them!?

> However, there was one thing still lacking. He needed to be anointed.

Go, set My people free!

Although he was different and had changed; and though he was a better person than he was forty

years prior, He had to have the anointing. He had to have the presence of Almighty God with him.

When the Lord said to Moses, "Go...," He anointed him.
And the Lord spake unto Moses, "Go unto Pharaoh, and say unto him, 'Thus saith the Lord, let my people go, that they may serve me.'" Exodus 8:1

"And he said unto them, 'go ye into all the world, and preach the gospel to every creature.'"
Mark 16:15

When you are sent by someone, you become their representative. This is regardless of the situation, purpose and reason for which you are sent. If you are sent, you have then become a representative. You are then an Ambassador.

If I send you to inquire for me about a certain thing of someone, you have just become my representative; my ambassador. You go in my name.

"Sir, David Ramiah would like to know if you are still interested in marketing his books."

You would return to inform me of the answer or questions from that person. I have given you power to represent me to that sales manager the moment that I said, "Go!"

The Lord said to Moses, "Go, set My people free!"

Moses must have thought, "I have been driven out once. This time they are going to kill me! Can't He just send someone else? Why does He have to bother with poor, little, old me? I am just going to stay here with my little flock, and live quietly right here in my humble desert. Someone better suited than me can set His people free. I tried once, look where it got me."

Furthermore, he wanted to know how the people would know that God sent him.

"Who am I going to say sent me?"

"Tell them 'I am that I am' sent you."

He was still trying to convince God not to send him. Finally the Lord asked him what he had in his hand. "Cast it down to the ground."

Lo and behold the rod became a snake. Can you see Moses leaping backwards away from the thing!?
"Take it up by the tail."

What was the Lord showing Moses in all of this?

"You are My representative now. I have given you power of attorney. You are My ambassador. And as such, you have been delegated with power to act in My name."

The Lord anointed Moses with miracle working power the very moment that He said to him, "Go!"

> "And Moses answered and said, 'But behold, they will not believe me, nor hearken unto my voice: For they will say, the Lord hath not appeared unto thee.' And the Lord said unto him, 'What is that in thy hand?' And he said, 'A rod.'
> And He said, 'Cast it on the ground.' And he cast it on the ground, and it became a serpent; and Moses fled from before it.
>
> And the Lord said unto Moses, 'Put forth thine hand, and take it by the tail:' And he put forth his hand, and caught it, and it became a rod in his hand: That they may believe that the Lord God of their fathers, the God of Abraham, the God of Isaac, and the God of Jacob, hath appeared unto thee." Exodus 4:1-5
>
> "And Moses said unto the Lord, 'O my Lord, I am not eloquent, neither heretofore, nor since Thou hast spoken unto Thy servant: But I am slow of speech, and of a slow tongue.' And the Lord said unto him, 'Who hath made man's mouth? Or who maketh the dumb, or the deaf,

or the seeing, or the blind? Have not I, the Lord? Now therefore go, and I will be with thy mouth, and teach thee what thou shalt say.'

And he said, 'O my Lord, send, I pray thee, by the hand of whom thou wilt send.' And the anger of the Lord was kindled against Moses, and he said, 'Is not Aaron the Levite thy brother? I know that he can speak well. And also, behold, he cometh forth to meet thee: And when he seeth thee, he will be glad in his heart.

And thou shalt speak unto him, and put words in his mouth: And I will be with thy mouth, and with his mouth, and will teach you what ye shall do. And he shall be thy spokesman unto the people: and he shall be, even he shall be to thee instead of a mouth, and thou shalt be to him instead of God. And thou shalt take this rod in thine hand, wherewith thou shalt do signs.'"

Exodus 4:10-17

Miracle Working Power

Moses approaches Pharaoh with his side kick Aaron.
He speaks to Pharaoh and asks him to let the slaves
go. Pharaoh, every prince and princess; man and
woman: his servants, soldiers, entertainers, every
scribe, enchanter and wise man in the throne room,
laughed Moses to scorn.

With head hanging low he slowly looked
around the room, and then at his brother.

Suddenly, a force surged through him like a
volcano and he roared out, "Your water shall turn to
blood!"

Time and time again he went to Pharaoh,
and Pharaoh refused to let the people go. And
again they laughed and scorned Moses. "A multitude
of frogs shall come upon your land!"

Again and again, Moses stood before
Pharaoh and *declared* the plagues of God that
would come upon Egypt. And they came. It took
place just like the man of God *spoke*. After the ninth
plague, Pharaoh was still adamant. He would not let
God's people go. But there was still one more
plague to come.

This time Pharaoh was going to feel the pain
of losing a child. This time he was going to face the
same pangs and torture; he was going to

experience the very same anger and loss that Israel faced, when Pharaoh's father killed the first born sons of the Jews, of two years old and under.

Moses, was one of those little ones destined to be killed, but the Lord miraculously saved him.

He was hidden and raised in Pharaoh's Palace by Pharaoh's own sister. While he was yet a child and destined to die, God saved him. And now, the Lord was using him to deliver Israel from bondage.

The last plague came. Every firstborn son and daughter of Egypt died. Not only did they lose their children, but every firstborn cattle that they had in the land died also.

Pharaoh finally succumbs. "Take your people and go from me."

> "And Moses said unto the people, 'Remember this day, in which ye came out from Egypt, out of the house of bondage; for by strength of hand the Lord brought you out from this place...'" Exodus 13:3

Still under the "Go" Anointing

With songs of praise on their lips and ecstatic joy in their heart, they marched proudly out of Egypt. Israel was free!

Two million or more, they marched behind the man of God.

Dust lifted around their feet. Laughter of children filled the air. Joy and gladness overwhelmed their hearts. And a great expectation of a new life filled their soul. Israel was rejoicing!

But, there was a great big obstacle in the way.

The Red sea lay sprawled between them and their promised land. How were they going to get to the other side?

There were no ships around. And even if there were any, there wouldn't have been enough to take even a million people across. What was Moses going to do?

"Lord, what am I going to do?"

"Stretch the rod over the sea!"

Suddenly, a most powerful wind blew. It divided the sea. The water separated and became a wall on both sides. The ground dried up and the people of Israel walked right across to the other side, carrying all their possessions with them.

By this time Pharaoh was enraged. He had lost his son and his slaves; all in the same day! This cannot be! He couldn't let this happen. What would the world say about the great Pharaoh?

He gathered his army.

Egyptian desert sand churned by the wheels of speeding chariots formed dust clouds. Pharaoh charged hard after the people.

Rattling and clanging armour, the yells and screams of soldiers, and the sound of galloping hooves filled the air.

The King was going to bring his prized treasure back to Egypt!

In the meantime the people of Israel were already arriving on the other side of the sea.

But there were no hesitations in Pharaoh. He was going to get his slaves back no matter what it took. The people of Israel were not going to get away.

Into the great divide Pharaoh's army charged. They poured into the passage between the walls of water. And the walls of water came crashing down.

Soldiers, horses and chariots were suddenly and quickly under water. They perished. In no time, the entire army disappeared.

Pharaoh's formidable force was lost. Egypt was broken.

Not only did Pharaoh lose his first born son, the first born children of his people, the first born of his cattle and flocks, he also lost his army and his precious slaves; all in one day!

Who is going to protect and fight for Egypt? Who is going to gather in the crops and build his barns and buildings? Who is going to nurse the children of his people and carry them on their backs? Who is going to plant his crops and build his roads?

Egypt has come to nothing.

Power of the Go Anointing

God gave a command to Moses, "Go and set My people free!"

That command provided Moses with all the anointing of God that he needed to fulfill the very mandate and purpose of God.

He freed the Israelites under that anointing! He brought them right out of Egypt and even divided a sea for them to cross over. Can you imagine what a double portion of that anointing would do?

> "And the Lord said unto Moses, 'Wheretofore criest thou unto Me? Speak unto the children of Israel, that they may go forward: But lift thou up thy rod, and stretch out thine hand over the sea and divide it: And the children of Israel shall go on dry ground through the sea. And I, behold, I will harden the hearts of the Egyptians, and they shall follow them: And I will get me honour upon Pharaoh, and upon all his host, upon his chariots, and upon his horsemen.'
>
> And the angel of God, which went before the camp of Israel, removed and went behind them; and the pillar of the cloud went from before their face, and stood behind them: And it came between the camp of the Egyptians and the camp of Israel; and it was a cloud and darkness to them, but it gave light by night to these: So that the one came not near the other all the night."
>
> Exodus 14:15-20

Points to reconsider and ponder

- It is about calling and anointing!

- God will not choose someone else.

- God has placed in you exactly what he needs to get the job done.

- *What you need to fulfill your call in life, is already in your hands.*

- Moses needed to be anointed.

- "Go and set My people free!" That command provided Moses with all the anointing of God that he needed to fulfill the very mandate and purpose of God.

- If God calls you, He will anoint you.

Chapter Two

Empty Vessels

How can I have more of the anointing?

How can I receive more power?

In what way can I be filled to a greater capacity with God's anointing?

By what means can I do the works of Jesus Christ?

How can I be more effective in ministry?

How can I experience more of the presence of the Lord?

Is there a way that I can see more lives affected and changed for Jesus?

All over the world believers are asking these very same questions.

Christians want more of God and desire a greater anointing. And in most cases they do not necessarily want that anointing so that they can use it to their own advantage, but for the benefit of others. What a remarkable and fantastic desire! The purpose of being able to be used of God in a more powerful and effective way, for the benefit of others, is marvelous. This is such an unselfish and wonderful desire. Undoubtedly, God will grant such a request!

To be used by God for the profit of other people is truly an outstanding and godly thing. The Lord will always grant such unselfish goals when applied with faith.

However, to want or to simply desire greater anointing is not sufficient.

However, to want or to simply desire greater anointing is not sufficient. To want greater anointing for any purpose is not enough. It is necessary that it be a whole hearted yearning to receive more and even greater anointing from God. It has to be a burning desire that causes you to hunger and thirst for more and more of Him. It must be a longing that causes you to seek Him with all of your heart, mind, and strength.

Most people answer, "Yes," When they are asked, "Do you want more of God?" But, they do not seek after and chase after the Lord with a fierce passion. They do not diligently and persistently pursue Him. In other words they go after Him this way: "I want more of God and if I receive more of Him, fine, and if not, well..."

In order to receive more of God you must desire Him with all your heart! You must want Him more than anything else in this world. You must diligently seek Him with all of your heart and soul.

In order to receive more of God you must desire Him with all your heart!

A Mother's Cry

"Now there cried a certain woman of the wives of the sons of the prophets unto Elisha, saying, 'Thy servant my husband is dead; and thou knowest that thy servant did fear the Lord: And the creditor is come to take unto him my two sons to be bondmen.' And Elisha said unto her, 'What shall I do for thee? Tell me, what hast thou in the house?'

And she said, 'Thine handmaid hath not anything in the house, save a pot of oil.'

Then he said, 'Go, borrow thee vessels abroad of all thy neighbours, even empty vessels; borrow not a few. And when thou art come in, thou shalt shut the door upon thee and upon thy sons, and shalt pour out into all those vessels, and thou shalt set aside that which is full.'

So she went from him, and shut the door upon her and upon her sons, who brought the vessels to her; and she poured out. And it came to pass, when the vessels were full, that she said unto her son, 'Bring me yet a vessel.'

And he said unto her, 'There is not a vessel more.' And the oil stayed. Then she came and told the man of God.

And he said, 'Go, sell the oil, and pay thy debt, and live thou and thy children of the rest.'"

2nd Kings 4: 1- 7

What does this story have to do with wanting more of God? What does it have to do with seeking Him diligently and with all your heart? What does it have to do with greater anointing? Let us examine.

The wife of a dead prophet came to Elisha and said to him, "The creditor has come to take my sons away for debts I owe."

Can you imagine what it would feel like to be losing your sons for debts owed, that you couldn't pay? Can you imagine how desperate, how destitute, and how afraid this woman must have been? To lose her sons after she had already lost her beloved husband!? The creditor is coming to take away her sons! What a tragedy this situation poses.

How would you react? How would you face such a tragic situation?

One great thing about it is that she had someone to go to. She was able to speak to the man of God and to get advice.

I know that there are those who think that they can handle anything and anybody. Some people do not wish for others to know what they are suffering or going through. But, in times like these I believe that you will seek out someone to talk to. You will search for answers in your desperate situation. And you will desire help to get you out of the disastrous corner you find yourself in. It is important to receive advice on your problems and situations.

Still, what does this have to do with receiving greater anointing?

The prophet's wife sought after the man of God. Elisha asked her "What shall I do for you? What do you have in the house?"

"A pot of oil" she replied.

Why did Elisha ask the woman the second question in the same instance? Why did he ask her about her possessions?

Elisha knew the answer to his own questions before he asked them. He knew that whatever the woman had in her house could be multiplied to meet her needs. And he knew that there had to be something in her house; something in her possession, that God could use to work a miracle for her.

People often assume that somehow the Lord will just drop their needs out of heaven for them. Sometimes they think that He is going to send an angel, and the angel will perform a miracle on the spot. Then again they may imagine that while they are sitting in their homes doing nothing, God will show up with a basket of food or a sack of money to meet their need.

All of this is possible! However, the Lord in the majority of cases uses the person who is in the middle of the situation to work the miracle. Though, there are times when He will use other people as well.

He knew that
whatever the woman
had in her house
could be multiplied
to meet her needs.

You may remember the story of Israel when they came out of Egypt. God said to Moses, "What do you have in your hand?" After he answered, the Lord said to him to lift the rod over the Red sea — Exodus 14: 16. A miracle took place!

> You have in your hands
> what is needed for a
> miracle to take place in
> your life!

Miracle in your hand

You have in your hands what is needed for a miracle to take place in your life! In you, in your life, Jehovah has placed the working of a miracle. What is it? What do you possess that God desires to work a miracle with? You will have to find out!

Ask the Lord, "Jesus, what do I have in my hands for you to bring me out of this poverty? What is it that I possess that you are going to use to set me free from this bondage? Where is the rod in my life that you are waiting for me to lift up, so that you will work a miracle for me? Which part of my possessions have you specifically given to me that you will multiply and increase to meet my needs?"

It could be a talent, it could be a gift. It is possible that it is an inheritance; a piece of property or an heirloom. Maybe it is your great insight into the things of God. Perhaps it is the education that you have gained through your studies. Then again it may be none of the above. Possibly, it is just simple little old you. You may think that you have nothing. But nothing plus Jesus is everything! You can do all things through Christ who strengthens you!

Once you have found out what the Lord has placed in you or in your life, so that He can perform miracles for you, you will have to act precisely according to His instructions. After you have done what the Lord has told you to do, you will see great and wonderful things take place in your life. And do not despise the little things either. They are stepping stones for the big things. They are steps on a ladder that will take you to the heavens.

God's Heavenly Provision

Jehovah rained down manna from heaven for Israel. But the people had to gather enough for each household every day. When He brought quails and caused them to fall by the camp, they likewise had to gather them up. Israel played a part in each instance. They had to contribute.

You likewise will have to contribute something to solve your problem. You must also share in the act of receiving your miracle. It might be your money, your bread, your water, your gift and talent, your time and energy, or something else that you possess that the Lord would require to perform the miracle for you.

Jesus told Peter to cast a hook into the sea and catch a fish. He then found gold in the fish's mouth to pay the tax. When Jesus made wine at the wedding feast, the servants had to obey Him and fill the containers with water. Naaman had to obey the servant of God, and he had to dip seven times in the Jordan River to receive his healing.

Five thousand men plus women and children were fed by the multiplication of loaves and fishes. However, if the little boy hadn't been willing to give his loaves and fishes, there wouldn't have been a miracle that day.

Soldiers dug ditches at the command of Elisha in the days of Jehoshaphat, according to 2nd Kings Chapter 3. The next morning, the ditches were filled with water even though it didn't rain that night. It looked like blood from a distance to the enemy soldiers. They decided to attack, and they were totally annihilated by the armies of Israel and Judah.

Jesus may ask you to dig a ditch!

What do you possess that God could multiply for you? What is it that you have that God could use to work a miracle for you? Is there something that you are holding in your hands right now that God could multiply for you? Can you believe Him today to perform a miracle for you? Would you do anything that He tells you to do, so that He could work a miracle for you to change your situation?

You likewise will have to contribute something to solve your problem.

Each one of us has something that God could use to work a miracle! And we need to find out what that thing is. You need to find out for yourself. It is necessary that you ask the Lord to show you. There must be one thing that you possess which He can increase for you. He will show you what it is if you ask Him.

Multiplication

The dead prophet's wife knew where to go for help. When she went to the man of God, she was asked, "What do you have?" She was then told what to do with what she had, and when she did, she experienced a miracle!

Every person has needs. Some people have debts that need to be paid. Personally, you may have a lack and do not know what to do, where to turn to, or how to have those needs met. You may have sought God, but along the way, you have lost faith. Perhaps you have just given up. God is saying to you today, "What do you have in your house? What do you have in your possession that I can multiply for you? I want to help you meet your needs!"

It could be money, a gift, a talent or ability; a job, your business, or your profession. It could be a servant's heart. What is it? God wants to increase it. But first, you must know what it is.

The Pot of Oil

When the dead prophet's wife said to Elisha, "I have a pot of oil," he gave her an instruction. He specifically instructed her as to what to do to receive her miracle. *He directed her to work with what she had.* He told her to do three things: Borrow all the empty vessels that you can; take your container of oil; and then fill all the empty ones that you have borrowed.

Wow! What a revelation. I never saw this truth in *this story*, before today. And right now as I write to you -April 11th, 2008 at 4.10 pm- God revealed it to me. It is so clear in so many other places in the Bible. But here it is also; the more you give, the more you will receive.

When the woman took her container of oil and followed the instructions of Elisha, her problem was solved. Her situation was changed forever. One thing! That was all that it took. All that was needed was a little insignificant bottle of oil and obeying the man of God! The container of oil never emptied until all the borrowed containers were filled.

The more you give, the more you will receive.

"So she went from him, and shut the door upon her and upon her sons, who brought the vessels to her; and she poured out. And it came to pass, when the vessels were full, that she said unto her son, 'Bring me yet a vessel.'

And he said unto her, 'There is not a vessel more.' And the oil stayed. Then she came and told the man of God.

And he said, 'Go, sell the oil, and pay thy debt, and live thou and thy children of the rest.'"

2nd Kings 4: 1- 7

What do you have in your hands that the Lord can multiply for you to meet all of your needs? What do you have in your possession? God is waiting for you to present it to Him.

And yet still, what does this have to do with receiving greater anointing?

Points to reconsider and ponder

- In order to receive more of God you must desire Him with all your heart!

- He knew that whatever the woman had in her house could be multiplied to meet her needs.

- You have in your hands what is needed for a miracle to take place in your life!

- You likewise will have to contribute something to solve your problem.

- The more you give, the more you will receive.

"YOU CANNOT CHANGE YESTERDAY. HOWEVER, TOMORROW'S OUTCOME WILL SURELY BE AFFECTED BY THE DECISIONS YOU MAKE TODAY."

Chapter Three

God's Instructions Followed

Do not leave any rock unturned when searching for something in your life that God can perform a miracle with. It might be very insignificant and little. It might seem to be worth nothing. But, do not disregard it! It might be the one thing that God is looking for. You see, in the first place, it is He who placed it there.

If you want a miracle from God, if you desire multiplication in your life; if you wish to have more in your life, you will then need to find that special something that you possess and present it to the Lord! You may have more than one. If that is the case present them all to the Lord. And when He instructs you, believe and obey. You will have your miracle.

At present, I have two other books that are already published, "The Power is Yours," and "What You Weren't Told About Righteousness." These two books I have placed into the hands of Jesus, and I have said, "Lord, this is what I have in my hands, multiply them."

While I am waiting for the Lord to multiply the sales of the books, and place them into the hands of the multitudes that need them, I am not sitting down and waiting for God to do everything. I have been meeting with people, discussing methods and strategies, and walking through every door that is opening. Soon, I will see the multiplication in Jesus' name. Amen!

The most important thing is that God has given to me some wonderful truths to share with others. And I desire that everyone would receive these revelations. This is because I know that their lives will be impacted, resulting in positive, fruitful, and wonderful change.

When you present to God what you want Him to multiply, He will instruct you. He will tell you what to do with whatever you have. And at that moment, you will have to believe the Lord and obey Him! You will need to do exactly what He tells you to do. You must do your part, and he will do His. You cannot sit at home, do nothing and say, "Here God, multiply this." It might not be multiplied! *You will have to act on the precise instructions of the Lord before it happens.*

When you present to God what you want Him to multiply, He will instruct you.

What did the prophet's wife do? She did exactly what Elisha told her to do. What did the disciples of Jesus do when He told them to let the multitude sit down? What did they do when He said to take the bread and fish and give them to the people? They did exactly what He told them to do! The entire multitude was fed with the multiplication of five loaves and two fishes.

There will be times that you will have to surrender certain things in your life. Some things may have to go before you will experience breakthroughs and miracles in your life. But, you need to do whatever the Lord tells you to do! You must act on God's direction and instructions.

It is possible that you might have to go out and get a job. Here you can use your gifts and talents which the Lord will multiply and increase to your benefit, as well as for others. You may have to venture out and set up a business. You might have to start a ministry, a church, an outreach program or some other work. But there will be something special that God will tell you to do. It will take your obedience and your faith to see the multiplication and miracle.

Receiving God's Servants

The prophet's wife believed the man of God and obeyed Him. She borrowed empty vessels from all her neighbours. She borrowed as many containers as she could; not just a few. Then she shut the door and began pouring the oil.

She followed the
instructions of the man
of God to the letter!

What did she do? She followed the instructions of the man of God to the letter! She first went out and got the containers. She brought them home and shut the door behind her and her sons. No one it seems was to know about what was going on in that house. When the door was closed, she began to fill up the empty containers with the oil. Because she believed, and because she obeyed the man of God, she received her miracle!

> "He who receives you receives Me, and he who receives Me receives Him who sent Me. He who receives a prophet in the name of a prophet, shall receive a prophet's reward. And he who receives a righteous man in the name of a righteous man, shall receive a righteous man's reward."
> Matthew 10:41 NKJV

According to how you receive a man or woman of God, that is how you will receive from them what the Lord has placed inside of them.

According to how you receive a man or woman of God, that is how you will receive from them what the Lord has placed inside of them. The anointing, their gifts and the presence of Holy Spirit in their life will flow into yours, but, only according to how you receive them.

Have you ever wondered why in some instances people who are sick are not healed? Someone may put their hands on them and pray for them, but they are not healed. However, the same person may lay his hands on others and they are instantly healed. Why? One reason is because of how that man or woman of God is received by the one who is sick or needing answers to prayers.

It is the same as an empty vessel that you would pour water into. If the cover is off, the vessel will be filled. If the cover is on, the water will be spilled.

In this case, when a servant of God is not received as one who is anointed by God, with the power of Jesus Christ flowing in their life to heal the sick, the sick are hardly healed. They are not able to draw from that anointed one of God the virtues invested in him or her.

The dead prophet's wife submitted herself to Elisha, and received from his life the presence, the power, and the anointing of God. If you receive a prophet as a prophet, you will be rewarded accordingly!

God Working Miracles

I have travelled and ministered in various parts of Brazil. I have travelled on the Amazon River, the

Solomois River, and the Black River. Mission boats carry doctors and nurses, dentists, evangelists and other ministry workers to provide medical and dental help to the natives. They live in little villages along the banks of these rivers. Services are held on the boats or in churches that were built by the Central Presbyterian Church of Manaus. Their pastor is José João Mesquita. This church has the largest boat ministry in Brazil that I know of.

Whilst I was in Brazil for ministry in February of 2003, I travelled on the Amazon River aboard the mission boat, "Zany Silva." Throughout the mission trip and during my stay in Manaus, I saw God move like I have never seen Him move before in my life. Everywhere I went, when I laid hands on people and prayed for them, they were healed.

A ten year old boy was healed of Asthma; a woman was healed of an enlarged aorta; and many others were healed of pain in their bodies and other sicknesses. In every service, the power of God was present in a mighty way. People came weeping to the altars repenting before the Lord. Some were weeping for joy in the presence of the Lord while others were baptized in the Holy Spirit. You can read more about these healings in my book, "What You Weren't Told About Righteousness."

Obedience

If I hadn't obeyed God and gone to Brazil, none of the things that happened there would have taken place. I believed the Lord and obeyed Him. I presented to Him, His call on my life; I presented to Him, His anointing in my life; I presented to Him the oil of God in my life, and I said, "Let it be poured into the lives of others."

I did not stay home and ask the Lord to multiply what I had. I went to where He was leading me to go, and I said, "Here I am Lord, use me."

Every empty vessel that came to be ministered to was filled. People were saved and sanctified by the blood of Jesus. They were healed and delivered, and baptized in the Holy Spirit. As long as there were empty vessels, the oil of God in my life poured out into them. It did not stop flowing until all needs were met. It was an awesome thing to behold.

Are you submissive to your pastor? Do you respectfully and submissively go to him for prayer and counsel in your time of need? **According to how you receive your pastor is how the anointing in his life will flow to yours.** In the way that you accept him, is how the blessing of God from him will pass on to your life.

The Empty Vessels

As long as the woman who came to the prophet had empty vessels to fill, the oil flowed. When all the vessels were filled, the oil stopped flowing. She then sold the abundance of oil that was multiplied for her. She paid off her debts, and for the rest of her entire life, she lived on what was left over.

You are also a vessel. As long as you are being poured out into the lives of others, you yourself will always be filled!

As long as you are being poured out into the lives of others, you yourself will always be filled!

That brings us to what I began to say to you. You may desire more of God, and perhaps you want to share the Lord with the entire universe. You can have greater anointing in order to do this! You can receive a greater measure of the presence of God.

However, to receive more of Him you will have to want Him above everything else in your life. You will have to desire Him with all your heart. It is only those that seek Him diligently and with all their hearts who will find Him.

> "But if from thence thou shalt seek the LORD thy God, thou shalt find *him*, if thou seek him with all thy heart and with all thy soul."
>
> Deuteronomy 4:29

Be an Empty Vessel before God

But, you must not only want Him more than anything else in life. You must come to Him empty. It is only into empty vessels that He will be poured.

Can you pour anything into a vessel that is full? Would you try filling a container that is already filled up to the brim with something else? You wouldn't try pouring into a pot that is covered would you?

Can you imagine the oil of God being poured into vessels that are full with other things? Can it be dispensed into containers that are full of pride and arrogance? Could the power of God be poured into a vessel that is filled with religious pride? How can the Spirit of the Lord rain down upon or into a vessel that is full of the pride of life, lust of the flesh, lust of the eyes, selfishness, greed, unforgiveness, bitterness, anger, hate and every other ungodly thing that you can imagine?

The Vessel has to be made empty. Or at least approach God, and desire of Him to enable you to be emptied of all these things. He will grant you such a desire.

To receive more of God you must first be emptied of all hindrances. Take the cover off of your heart and soul. What could that cover be? It could be pride and ego; a root of bitterness; unforgiveness, hate and malice, disobedience, rebellion, anger or some other similar thing. Possibly, it is fear and doubt. Find out what it is and remove it.

All hindrances have to be removed in order to receive more of the Lord. To receive greater anointing you must be empty of the above things. They are like the boulders, rocks and debris that clog up wells. They are blocking the flow of the Spirit of God in your life. The life giving, Holy Spirit water of life cannot flow from your spirit into your soul and body. The well is clogged. It has to be unclogged!

After you have cleared your well; after you have removed the boulders, rocks and debris, God will pour more of His presence into you and fill you up to overflowing. Then you will break forth into joy

But, you must not only want Him more than anything else in life. You must come to Him empty.

and rejoicing like never before! Then you will see the power of God at work in you to change lives. And then He will cause His blessing to flow in your life in a greater measure. And that is when, as you pour into the lives of others, the Lord will pour more of His anointing into you.

To Be Empty

How do you empty yourself?

During this same time that I was in Brazil, there was a certain woman at one of the meetings who desired more of God. She asked me to pray that she would receive more of the Lord. Usually when people make such a request, they are seeking and asking for greater anointing.

We were at a camp ground, and we were standing out in the open. It was starting to get dark. Those that were there gathered to me and asked me to minister to them. As they came together encircling me, I told them to begin to talk to the Lord; to simply worship Him and tell Him their needs. As they did, young and old alike began to weep. And I started to pray for them.

Rai was standing to my left and holding my left hand. As she sought the Lord, she began to weep. Sobbing uncontrollably, she poured her heart out to Jesus, and tears cascaded down her face like rain off of a roof. She needed more of Him.

It has been a very long time since I saw anyone weep before God and cry out to Him like this. Almost exactly one year later, I not only saw it, but experienced it in my own life in another City of Brazil. That was when I wept for almost three hours, and prayed with all of my heart for the poor of the City of Uberlandia.

Rai wept before the Lord and called out to Him with all of her heart. Tears streamed down her face as she sobbed and lamented. She wept before God, calling upon the name of our Lord and Saviour Jesus Christ. At the same time, she held on to my arm and gripped it with all of her strength.

As she sobbed and sobbed, slowly - very slowly - she lowered her knees to the ground. I held up her weight as her knees slowly bowed to the ground. Tears tumbled down her face. Sobbing and groaning from the depths of her soul, she faced her Maker with a broken and a contrite heart. She wept and pleaded with the Lord for more of Him in her life.

Everyone saw and everyone heard. But she wasn't afraid of what others would say. She wasn't concerned about what they might think. She desired with all of her heart to have more of God, and that was all that mattered.

Pride was dispelled! Religion was dead! And every ungodly thing that might have held her back was defied. Only one thing mattered, *"More of You Lord, more of You."*

She humbled and emptied herself so that she could be filled with more of the presence of Holy Spirit. She knew she couldn't go on with *just enough.* Recognizing that she needed a richer and greater presence of God in her life, this wonderful woman was willing to do whatever was necessary. Are you willing to do whatever is necessary to receive greater anointing from Jesus?

God will not despise a broken and contrite spirit:

"The sacrifices of God are a broken spirit, a broken and a contrite heart, O God, Thou wilt not despise." Psalm 51:17

That night, Rai received from Jesus what she so greatly desired. She obtained exactly what she needed from Him! But only because she emptied herself of all the other stuff that she was full of. If you desire more of the Spirit of God to fill your soul, heart and mind, you will have to do the same.

Submitting oneself to God's anointed servant

Another thing that is vitally important to notice is that when the people of Manaus said to me, "David, minister to us," they were open to the Spirit of God and His anointing upon my life to flow into theirs. And according to how they received me, they received from the Lord.

> "He that receiveth you receiveth me, and he that receiveth me receiveth him that sent me. He that receiveth a prophet in the name of a prophet shall receive a prophet's reward; and he that receiveth a righteous man in the name of a righteous man shall receive a righteous man's reward.
>
> And whosoever shall give to drink unto one of these little ones a cup of

cold *water* only in the name of a disciple verily I say unto you, he shall in no wise lose his reward."

Matthew 10:41

If it was that they received me as a prophet, then they received a prophet's reward. If it was as a righteous man, then they received a righteous man's reward. If they received me as a pastor, evangelist, teacher or apostle, they received their reward accordingly.

In whatever measure that you see and accept your pastor, elder, or any other minister of God, it is in that measure that you will receive whatever God has placed in them for you. If you receive a minister of the Lord as someone who is anointed and is a representative of His, and you believe that God can bring deliverance, healing and other blessings through him or her, you will have those needs met.

The fivefold ministry has been put here by God for the above purpose - to edify and build up the Body of Christ. The Lord made sure that His people would be taken care of. Therefore, you are to be open to the ministers of Jesus with **discernment**. When you do, you will receive His power and anointing, and His wisdom and blessing that He has placed in their lives for you.

Receiving Oil

There are many people who need to humble and empty themselves like Rai. Perhaps you are one of them. Are you willing to empty yourself of all the hindrances? Are you ready to do whatever it would take to be emptied of every evil blockade in your life? Are you ready and willing to get rid of any and all debris, rock and boulders that may be in you? If you are, you will be filled.

All over the world, there are Christians who desire more of God, but they are not willing to empty themselves. They are not eager to put the effort and work into removing the hindrances that are in their lives. *God is not going to do the work for you!* You will have to present your life to Jesus like Rai. Then you will have to empty yourself of the boulders, rocks and debris that your life is full of. You will have to, in order to be filled up with more of Jesus.

Only empty vessels will be filled! Every empty vessel was filled in the house of the woman who was instructed by Elisha. When all were filled, the oil stopped. Empty yourself that you may be filled with more.

Why should you want to be filled up with more of God?

Points to reconsider and ponder

- When you present to God what you want Him to multiply, He will instruct you. She followed the instructions of the man of God to the letter!

- According to how you receive a man or woman of God, that is how you will receive from them what the Lord has placed inside of them.

- As long as you are being poured out into the lives of others, you yourself will always be filled!

- But, you must not only want Him more than anything else in life. You must come to Him empty.

Chapter Four

Extra Oil

With sufficient oil, a lamp will burn brightly and for the entire night. Lamps with enough oil can be put out, yet, be ready when you are to light them up again.

Your life is similar to a lamp. You can be filled to capacity with the oil of Holy Spirit. And you can be burning brightly all night and every day for the rest of your life. You would be brilliantly shining and give light to all those around you. Everywhere you go; people would see the glory of Jesus Christ upon your life and praise the Lord for it.

However, if you do not have enough oil of the Holy Spirit, your light will be just a flicker.

That is why it is so important that you be filled up with more oil of the Spirit of God on a daily basis. What do I mean when I say, "If you do not have enough oil of the Holy Spirit"?

When you receive Christ as your personal Lord and Saviour, Holy Spirit who is the Spirit of God and the Spirit of Christ, comes to reside on the inside of your spirit. From there He flows into your soul and will be evident in your life.

But, when your soul is full of all kinds of hindrances like we shared in the previous chapters, the power of God and His anointing are limited in your life.

> "But ye are not in the flesh, but in the Spirit, if so be that the Spirit of God dwell in you. Now if any man have not the Spirit of Christ, he is none of his."
> Romans 8:9

> "Know ye not that ye are the temple of God, and *that* the Spirit of God dwelleth in you?"
> 1st Corinthians 41:16

If your well of living water is plugged up with boulders, rocks and debris, there might only be a trickle of life coming from it. The well that is in your spirit therefore, needs to be unplugged before the life giving force in it can flow. And so the oil of Holy

Spirit in your soul must be replenished every day. It must be brought up from your spirit into your soul, just like one would bring water up out of a well with a bucket. When that happens, you will be a great lamp, burning brilliantly bright and lighting up the world wherever you go.

> "Then shall the Kingdom of heaven be likened unto ten virgins, which took their lamps, and went forth to meet the bridegroom. And five of them were wise and five were foolish. They that were foolish took their lamps, and took no oil with them: but the wise took oil in their vessels with their lamps. While the bridegroom tarried, they all slumbered and slept. And at midnight there was a cry made, 'Behold the bridegroom cometh; go ye out to meet him.'
>
> Then all those virgins arose, and trimmed their lamps. And the foolish said unto the wise, 'Give us of your oil; for our lamps are gone out.'
>
> But the wise answered saying, 'Not so; lest there be not enough for us and you: But go ye rather to them that sell, and buy for yourselves.' And while they went to buy, the Bridegroom came; and they that

were ready went in with him to the marriage: And the door was shut. Afterward came also the other virgins, saying, 'Lord, Lord open to us.' But he answered and said, 'verily I say unto you, I know you not. Watch therefore, ye know neither the day nor the hour for wherein the Son of Man cometh.'"

Mathew 25:1-13

> These virgins did not
> represent a bride!!!

This is quite a unique picture that Jesus gives us of God's Kingdom. In this representation of God's Kingdom of which we are citizens, Jesus demonstrates that there are people who make wise decisions and there are those who make foolish decisions. This entire story is about being wise, and about making the correct decision to have sufficient oil that will last all night.

The ten virgins were part of a wedding party. When they arrived at the house of the wedding, they had to wait for the bridegroom to arrive. They would welcome him and then enter the house together with him. In this type of wedding, guests were required to meet the bridegroom outside of the house, and then enter the house together with him. Afterwards, the door was shut and those on the outside had to stay out.

The Bridegroom in this story was not going to be married to any of these virgins!

It is very important to recognize something very major here. This story is often used to teach people that the Body of Christ is the Bride of Christ. The Bridegroom in this story was not going to be married to any of these virgins! They were just part of the wedding party who met him outside of the house as he went to marry his bride. This story does not in any way shape or form tell us that the Body of Christ is the Bride of Christ.

The Bride of Christ:

> "And I John saw the holy city, new *Jerusalem*, coming down from God

out of heaven, *prepared as a bride*
adorned for her husband."

                               Revelations 21:2

"...Come hither, I will shew thee *the*
bride, the Lamb's wife. And he
carried me away in the spirit to a
great and high mountain, and
shewed me that great city, the *holy*
Jerusalem, descending out of heaven
from God."

                          Revelations 21:9, 10

Making wise decisions

These virgins were part of a group of people
waiting for a wedding celebration. We also are
waiting for a Bridegroom. We are waiting for The
Bridegroom - Jesus Christ. But, we are not waiting to
be married to Him! We are already one with Him.
We are His Body!

        The virgins in this story are examples of the
Body of Christ; they represent His Body. Five of
them were wise, and five of them were foolish.

        The wise virgins, in anticipation of the
bridegroom being late brought extra oil. The foolish
virgins in their anticipation; or in their failure to
calculate for him being late, did not come prepared.

They did not have extra oil. And thus, they were left on the outside.

The wise young women had a plan, so did the foolish ones. The wise ones planned to succeed, but the foolish planned to fail.

Being Wisely Prepared

As the Body of Christ we are also waiting for a Bridegroom - Jesus Christ.

In anticipation of Him being late, have you made plans? What are these plans? Plans to succeed or to fail? Have you brought with you extra oil? Have you brought any oil at all?

The wise were prepared. They had planned well. They had extra oil. They made the additional effort. They went the extra mile. And they reaped the reward.

Those who weren't smart decided that they were going to enter in on the shirt tails of the wise. They decided that if needed, they would get a little oil from those who had. Just in case they ran out of oil, and their lamps were going out, they were going to borrow from those whose lamps were burning brightly.

In the Kingdom of God, you cannot depend on someone else's oil. No one else's oil will keep you burning! You have to have your own. If you do not, your lamp will burn out. You will not have good success in life. And the rewards of having a brightly burning lamp that lights your way will not be yours.

> In the Kingdom of God, you cannot depend on someone else's oil.

Oil is a representative of Holy Spirit. It represents the unction or anointing of Holy Spirit. If you do not have this anointing, you cannot enter the house with the Bridegroom. You are going to be left on the outside. Jesus Christ is the anointed One and when we receive Him as our Lord and Saviour, we receive the anointing.

> "Then he remembered the days of old, Moses, *and* his people, *saying,* 'Where *is* he that brought them up out of the sea with the shepherd of

his flock?   Where *is* he that put his
Holy Spirit within him?'"

Isaiah 63:11

Relationship

The Kingdom of God in its entirety is a one to one
relationship with Jesus Christ. First and foremost, it is
all about relationship with Him.

You are not going to go to heaven because
your wife has a relationship with Jesus. You will not
go to heaven because your husband has a
relationship with Jesus. You are not going to go to
heaven because your father or your mother has a
relationship with the Lord. Neither will you go to be
with Him because your grandparents have a
relationship with Him. You will only get to heaven to
be with Jesus, and be there with Him for all eternity,
if you have a *personal relationship* with Him. It is one
to one, you and Him, and He and you.

If you have never asked Jesus Christ to be
your Lord and Saviour, pray this prayer and ask
Him.

Dear Father God, I thank you for
Jesus Christ. I recognize and
acknowledge that I have sinned.

> Please forgive me of all the sins I
> have committed and wash me with
> the blood of Jesus Christ. Jesus Christ,
> I invite you to come and live in my
> spirit so that I am born again. Father,
> today, I make Jesus Christ my Lord
> and my Saviour. Amen!

The Kingdom of God is not in observation; it is active, relational, and involved. When Jesus was questioned about the Kingdom of God by the Pharisees, this is what He said to them.

> "And when He was demanded of the
> Pharisees, when the Kingdom of God
> should come, He answered them and
> said, 'The kingdom of God cometh
> not with observation: Neither shall
> they say Lo here! Or, lo there! For,
> behold, the kingdom of God is within
> you.'"
>
>   Luke 17: 20, 21

Being part of God's Kingdom means to be involved in having a daily relationship with Jesus. Every day, spending time in the Word of God, in prayer, and time in praising and worshipping the Lord, brings you into deeper intimacy with Him. That is what I desire! Don't you?

Do not wait for a crisis or a time of crisis to arrive at your door to start praying. Start now! Do not wait for questions to arise, or situations and problems to occur before checking for what the Bible says; do it today. Study the Bible on a daily basis. Spend time in prayer every day. And praise and worship Jesus every free moment that you have. You will find yourself enveloped in His presence, captivated by His love, and supported by His sweet embrace.

    "Draw nigh to God, and He will draw nigh to you…"

James 4:8

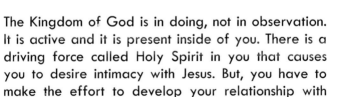

The Kingdom of God
in its entirety is a
one to one
relationship with
Jesus Christ.

The Kingdom of God is in doing, not in observation. It is active and it is present inside of you. There is a driving force called Holy Spirit in you that causes you to desire intimacy with Jesus. But, you have to make the effort to develop your relationship with Him. You need to make the decision to develop and strengthen your closeness with the Lord. You have to respond to the tug and pull of Holy Spirit.

In taking action and in making the effort to spend time with God; in prayer, in the word, in worship, and in drawing close to Him daily, you are being wise. You are being like the wise virgins who prepared for the long term. You are being like the wise young women who made plans to succeed. Like them you are prepared for a long wait if necessary.

No one knows when the Bridegroom will arrive. Therefore you have to always be ready. Suppose He delays like the bridegroom in this story? Let us assume that He does not come on the day that you are expecting Him to; do you have enough oil in your lamp to keep you burning until He comes? Or will your light go out before He arrives? Will you be empty and dry and turn away?

What will be for you on the day Jesus arrives? Will He find you still strong in faith? Are you going to be fully prepared, ready and waiting? Or will He find you dried up and dead like an empty river that is just full of sand and gravel? Will He find you to be just like bowls of dust blown about by the wind?

> Jesus said, "So then because thou art lukewarm, and neither cold nor hot, I will spew thee out of my mouth."
> Revelation 3:16

Paul said, "Quench not the Spirit."
1st Thessalonians 5:19

In other words do not dry up. You need fresh oil every day. Listen, a lamp only goes so long with so much oil. You then have to replenish the oil to keep the lamp burning.

The oil of the Holy Ghost is available to you free of charge! You do not have to go and buy it. You do not have to search for it. You do not have to borrow it. It is available to you right now!

Jesus said, "...For indeed the kingdom of God is within you." Luke 17:21

All you need to do is call upon Jesus Christ daily. All you need to do is draw nigh unto Him and He will draw nigh unto you. Study His word, worship Him daily, fast and pray, and fellowship with other believers in a Bible believing and Bible preaching church. Then, you will be like a tree planted by a river whose leaves never dry up, and whose fruits are abundant in season and out of season. Read more about developing closeness with Jesus, in my book: "The Power is Yours."

"Draw nigh to God, and He will draw nigh to you..." James 4:8

Where are you at today? Are you thirsty and dry? Are you hungry? Jesus said, *"Those that thirst and hunger after righteousness, will be filled."*

He said, "Seek ye first the Kingdom of God and His righteousness, and all other things will be added unto you." Matthew 6:33

What do you think? Do you believe that you need extra oil today? Do you need to be replenished? Is your lamp burning low? Is your vessel empty? It can be filled. Jesus is willing and able. He wants to fill you up today. Come to Him and allow Him to pour into you. And even if you are full, make sure and keep the level up! Are you ready to receive greater anointing?

Points to reconsider and ponder

- When you present to God what you want Him to multiply, He will instruct you.

- She followed the instructions of the man of God to the letter!

- You can be filled to capacity with the oil of Holy Spirit.

- The wise young women had a plan, so did the foolish ones. The wise ones planned to succeed, but the foolish planned to fail.

- In the Kingdom of God, you cannot depend on someone else's oil.

- The Kingdom of God in its entirety is a one to one relationship with Jesus Christ.

- The Kingdom of God is not in observation; it is active, relational, and involved.

- What will be for you on the day Jesus arrives? Will He find you still strong in faith? Are you going to be fully prepared, ready and waiting?

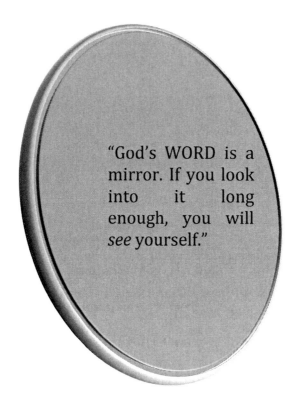

"God's WORD is a mirror. If you look into it long enough, you will *see* yourself."

Chapter Five

Living Water

When the woman said to the man of God, "I have a pot of oil," he gave her an instruction. It was precisely what she needed to do, to receive a miracle. He directed her to work with what she had. He told her three things: Borrow all the empty vessels that you can; take your container of oil and fill all the empty ones that you have borrowed.

"If you want to be filled with more, take what you have and pour it into the lives of others!"

Many times after I have preached, pastors and leaders would want to lay hands on me and pray for me. They believed that I have given out and therefore I must be refilled. They would pray for new strength and anointing to be given to me.

However, after I have ministered to a congregation I do not wish for anyone to pray for me like this. I do not need for anyone to pray and ask the Lord to refill me, refresh me or fill me with more anointing. Why? Please do not misunderstand.

When you understand the concept of giving and receiving, you know that you will receive more from the Lord when you give to others. You see, I am already refilled, refreshed and strengthened by Jesus Christ as I am pouring out to His people. It is the reason why I always feel stronger after powerful meetings of healing, deliverance and souls saved.

You must understand that it is God in me who is working, and giving, and healing, and working miracles through me. Not me! Therefore, as the power of God is flowing out of me, it is also flowing into me. This is because it is all of God. It all comes from Him, not from me. I am simply a conduit; a pipeline for Him to flow through. And as living water flows through me to others, I am watered myself. This is why, I do not desire for others to pray for me after I have ministered to people.

"For it is God which worketh in you both to will and to do of *his* good pleasure."

Philippians 2:13

The more that I give, the more it is that I receive. God does not leave me without strength afterwards. On the contrary! He fills me up as I give out of what is inside of me. And that is the anointing and power of Holy Spirit. Anything that God wants to give to his children through me is okay with me. He gives back more to me, as He pours out of Himself into others through me.

> Therefore, as the power of God is flowing out of me, it is also flowing into me.

However, in the first place I have to be obedient and willing for the Lord to work through me this way. I must make that first step and allow Him to operate through me. When I step out in faith to pray for someone, tell others about Jesus, visit people, give something to them, God does it through me. And according to how I give, it is also how I receive. Isn't that marvelous?!

Often I am more ready to go further after a great service. I am willing to pray for more people; ready to preach longer and minister some more. But, many times we are constrained by time. People have to go to work the next day. Some haven't had dinner yet. Others have to take their young children home to bed.

Yes, we do feel physically tired. We do, but the Spirit of the Lord strengthens us.

I always think, "Monday is for rest. On Sunday I am going to minister to God's children for as long as it takes."

The Bible says that according to how we give we will receive.

> "Give, and it shall be given unto you; good measure, pressed down, and shaken together, and running over, shall men give into your bosom. For with the same measure that ye mete withal it shall be measured to you again."
>
> Luke 6:38

Now, we most often think of this scripture in light of money. But, it is speaking of anything that we would give. Not just money. If you give your time to people, people will have time for you. If you are compassionate to the sick and needy, others will be compassionate to you. If you love people, you will be loved. According to how you give you will receive.

To receive greater anointing you must be willing to give out more from what you have. First, you must be empty of all hindrances: Evil thoughts, corrupted words, ungodly behaviour, etc. Then seek the Lord with all your heart. He will pour out His Spirit upon you and give you more anointing - more of His presence.

"If you want to be filled with more, take what you have and pour it into the lives of others!"

God does not want to be out there somewhere in the distance away from you. He desires to be right here with you. He wants you to understand that He will never leave you nor forsake you.

He loves you with an everlasting love. His love for you is unending. You cannot outrun His love, you cannot hide from His love, and you cannot out give His love.

When you recognize Him as Father; approach and relate to Him as such. Every day, more and more, you will find yourself in His arms.

You will find yourself sitting at His feet listening to every word He speaks. Sometimes sitting on His knees as He wraps his loving arms tenderly around you and tells you how much He loves you: Now and again walking hand in hand with Him along a garden path; sometimes sitting on a rock overlooking the shimmering lake, or lying under a tree. You listen as He describes Heaven and tells you what He has waiting there for you.

You find that every day, little by little, more and more, you are falling more in love with your Father. You are beginning to know Him. You are beginning to see Him for who He really is. You are starting to recognize the tenderhearted, loving, gentle, kind, compassionate, merciful and gracious Father that He is.

There is nowhere that you do not see Him. There isn't anywhere that you do not sense His presence. You find that He is always with you and truly never forsakes you. He is everywhere.

You feel the touch of His hand on your shoulder in the supermarket. He lets you know He is there. He talks with you in the car, in the bus, at the computer, and while you are studying. He speaks to you in dreams and in visions.

He speaks gently to you when you are walking along the street, while you are working and when you are with friends or family. He is with you always - He is your Father.

Can you feel His loving arms around you right now?

Taken from, "What You Weren't Told About Righteousness."

Are you starting to get hungry for greater anointing? I hope that you are.

Points to reconsider and ponder

- When the woman said to the man of God, "I have a pot of oil," he gave her an instruction. It was precisely what she needed to do, to receive a miracle.

- If you want to be filled with more, take what you have and pour it into the lives of others!

- When you understand the concept of giving and receiving, you know that you will receive more from the Lord when you give to others.

- Therefore, as the power of God is flowing out of me, it is also flowing into me.

Chapter Six

Spring of Life

While living among the Philistines, Isaac dug many wells. In the beginning, the Philistines accepted him and allowed him to live among them freely. However, as he began to increase and be blessed bountifully by the Lord, they despised him. They sought to drive him out of their midst and their land. One of the first things that they did was to fill up the wells which he depended on for sustenance. And when he dug new wells, the Philistines fought with him over the new wells.

There was a drought during the time that Isaac began to live among the Philistines. To sustain cattle, sheep, camels and donkeys, a man must have a sufficient supply of this life giving, life sustaining force; water. Water was the most expensive commodity in those days. A lack of water spells death and destruction. Having no water means no survival, no production, and no sustenance. You could not plant crops, you could not keep herds of cattle, and you could not maintain and keep your family alive. Isaac therefore, was in a very difficult situation.

He moved from one place to another, digging new wells. As fast as he would dig a well and settle in a new area however, the Philistines would quarrel with him over the wells, saying that the wells belonged to them. Isaac kept moving.

> "Also Isaac's servants dug in the valley, and found a well of running water there. But the herdsmen of Gerar quarrelled with Isaac's herdsmen, saying, 'The water is ours.' So he called the name of the well Esek, because they quarrelled with him. Then they dug another well, and they quarrelled over that one also. So he called its name Sitnah."

> Genesis 26:19 – 21

Prior to this he came to the place where His father Abraham had dug wells. He found that the Philistines had filled them up with earth.

> "The man began to prosper, and continued prospering until he became

very prosperous; for he had possessions of flocks and possessions of herds and a great number of servants. So the Philistines envied him. Now the Philistines had *stopped up* all the wells which his father's servants had dug in the days of Abraham his father, and they had filled them up with dirt."

Genesis 26:13 - 15

For Isaac to have water he had to clear the wells; he had to remove the earth, rock and debris from them. And when he did, the water began to flow again. He had sustenance for his flocks and family.

"And Abimelech said to Isaac, 'Go away from us, for you are much mightier than we.' Then Isaac departed from there and pitched his tent in the Valley of Gerar, and dwelt there.

And Isaac dug again the wells of water which they had dug in the days of Abraham his father, for the Philistines had stopped them up after the death of Abraham."

Genesis 26:16 -18

Isaac had to dig out the earth from the plugged up wells. He had to clear the wells so that the water might flow.

> "And he moved from there and dug another well, and they did not quarrel over it. So he called its name Rehoboth, because he said, 'For now the Lord has made room for us, and we shall be fruitful in the land.'"
>
> Genesis 26:22

Eventually, Isaac dug a well over which they did not quarrel. And finally, the Philistines left him alone. He flourished! His flocks, his family and his servants lived abundantly once again.

Reservoir

Under some wells there is a great big reservoir. You may dig a well and have an abundant supply of water. But if someone who hates you fills the well with boulders, rocks, dirt and debris, your water supply will be cut off. You will have no sustenance for your life. You and your family, your flocks and your servants will die!

What would you do? Where would you go? How would you react? Should you move about like

Isaac and dig new wells? You could! But, what would you do?

The thing is however, this is not the land of the Philistines, and this is not the ground that we are talking about. This is your spiritual life! Deep on the inside of you is a great big reservoir of abundant life giving water. It is there waiting for you to bring it to the surface.

Deep on the inside of you is a great big reservoir of abundant life giving water.

In an ordinary well, every time someone brings up a bucket of water from it, that bucket of water is replaced from the reservoir. The well is connected to the reservoir. It is the outlet that is hooked up to the main source. From this bountiful supply the well fills up in order to provide you with water.

In your spirit resides the source of living water. He is called Holy Spirit. He is your reservoir of life giving water. Every time that you reach down into your reservoir of living water through prayer, reading and studying the word, praising and worshiping Jesus Christ, and fellowshipping with other believers, you are filled up with more.

Whenever you bring up an ounce, a bucket full, or a barrel full of living water from your reservoir, it is replaced. You can never go dry. However, if you are not bringing any of it up, then your trees are going to die and you will bear no fruit. And if you bear no fruit, you are liable to be cut down like a dead branch and be thrown into the fire to be burned.

> "I AM the true vine, and my Father is the husbandman. Every branch in me that beareth not fruit he taketh away: And every *branch* that beareth fruit, he purgeth it, that it may bring forth more fruit. Now ye are clean through the word which I have spoken unto you. Abide in me, and I in you. As the branch cannot bear fruit of itself, except it abide in the vine; no more can ye, except ye abide in me.
>
> I am the vine, ye *are* the branches: He that abideth in me,and I in him, the same bringeth forth much fruit: For without me ye can do nothing. If a man abide not in me, he is cast forth as a branch, and is withered; and

men gather them, and cast *them* into
the fire, and they are burned."

John 15:1 – 6

Transformation

The five wise virgins brought extra oil along with
them just in case the bridegroom arrived late. He
did arrive late. But they went in to the house with
him because they had extra oil. Their lamps were
still burning! They had light! They were able to see
where they were going. Thus they followed him into
the house.

In your life today, you could experience the
riches of Christ's glory if you have sufficient oil in
your lamp.

What do I mean?

You are made up of three parts: Spirit, soul
and body. In your spirit is where Holy Spirit comes
to dwell. In your soul is where you feel; where you
think, love, hate; feel hunger, pain, anger, sorrow,
etc. And your body is what houses the two. Your
body is the dwelling place in which reside your spirit
and your soul. It is where you experience the results
of what is happening in your spirit and your soul.
That is why the Bible says:

"Beloved, I wish above all things that thou mayest prosper and be in health, even as thy soul prospereth." 3 John 2

Your soul and your body do not understand what your spirit understands. They did not experience what your spirit has experienced. Your spirit was transformed when you received Christ as your Lord and Saviour. It has become brand new!

"Behold old things have passed away, behold all things have become new."

2nd Corinthians 5:17

Your soul and your body do not understand what your spirit understands.

Now your flesh and your soul area need to understand and experience the same transformation. How can that happen? It will take place as you begin to take this powerful, life giving water from the well in your spirit, and bring it into the soul and flesh area. There, as you water the soul and the flesh, transformation takes place from glory to glory. As you bring this "water of life" that is in the depths of your spirit, into your soul and flesh area, new oil will keep your lamp burning brightly in Jesus!

How do you do that?

You must first remove the boulders, rocks, dirt and debris from your well. Isaac had to unclog the wells his father had dug which the Philistines had plugged up. If he hadn't, he would have died. He needed that life sustaining force. His flocks needed the water to live, his servants needed it to survive and stay alive, and so did his family.

Throughout life, you have been filled up with much debris, rocks and boulders. You think a certain way and you speak in a certain manner. You do things in a specific form. You have a special approach to life. However, if these ways are not God's ways, and if these thoughts are not God's thoughts; if these actions are not the way God would act, you have to get rid of them all!

> "God's ways are higher than your ways, His thoughts are higher than your thoughts." Isaiah 55: 8 -11

Like the wells of Isaac and his father which had to be unplugged, your well of life will have to be unplugged. Then the life giving; life sustaining Holy Spirit water from your innermost being will flow into your soul and body. It will result in abundance of life: Joy and happiness, health and wellness, gladness and joy in the presence of the Lord.

After you have cleared the way for the "water of life" to flow into your life, you will then have to bring it up to the surface into your soul and your flesh area. This will happen as you are praying, fasting, reading and studying the Bible daily, as you are praising and worshipping Jesus and fellowshipping with other Christians in a Bible believing church.

Now you are being wise like the wise virgins, who had extra oil for their lamps as they waited for the bridegroom.

But, we are not done yet! There is still more to come.

Points to reconsider and ponder

- But if someone who hates you fills the well with boulders, rocks, dirt and debris, your water supply will be cut off.

- Throughout life, you have been filled up with much debris, rocks and boulders.

- Like the wells of Isaac and his father which had to be unplugged, your *well of life* will have to be unplugged.

- Deep on the inside of you is a great big reservoir of abundant life giving water.

- In your spirit resides the source of living water. He is called Holy Spirit. He is your reservoir of life giving water.

- Your body is the dwelling place in which reside your spirit and your soul. It is where you experience the results of what is happening in your spirit and your soul.

"IF YOU ARE
SATISFIED
WITH WHERE
YOU ARE,
YOU WILL
NEVER GET
TO WHERE
YOU WANT
TO BE."

Chapter Seven

Encounter Greater Anointing

Moses was anointed to go. He went and miracles followed. This is the kind of thing that the anointing does. It causes demonstrations of the power of God. No one can deny the operation of the presence of God in someone's life when it is there. Some may attach it to another power, but none can deny that it is present and that it works.

From the Red Sea to the desert the "Go" anointing brought the Israelites through. It provided water for them to drink, food from heaven for them to eat, defeated their enemies, kept the clothes on their backs strong, and kept them going for forty years.

But, there was a greater anointing to come. And it didn't come until the man of God had an encounter with his Creator in a most majestic and powerful way.

Moses had marvelous experiences with the Lord. He pleaded with God for the lives of the Israelites when they had worshiped the golden calf. He entreated the Lord to forgive them and not blot them out of His book. He mediated and brought the leaders of the people to meet the Lord at the foot of the mountain. Time and time again, Moses stood between the people and God; he pleaded for them. If he hadn't, they could have been annihilated by the Lord.

Finally, the man who had walked with God for years, and had found favour with the Lord, wanted more.

For you to have greater anointing, you need to have a desire for "more of God." And you must desire Him with all of your heart! Then, you have to ask the Lord for more of His presence in your life.

Moses said, "Lord, I want to see you."

In other words it was like this: "God, you and I have been friends for a long time, but you have never let me see your face once! What kind of a relationship is this? It is kind of one sided you know, Lord. You get to see my face at any time that you want. I never get to see yours."

It is not that Moses never saw the Lord's face. As a matter of fact, not only Moses, but seventy elders of Israel also saw God's face. And not only did they see the Lord's face, they ate with him. However, this was not the glorified face of God. Moses desired to see the Lord's glorified face.

God's glorious face is too powerful for any human to behold on this earth. They could not see the Lord's glorified face and live. Even Moses couldn't. So the Lord granted him to see His back and not His face.

> "And he said, 'I beseech thee, shew me thy glory.' And he said, 'I will make all my goodness pass before thee, and I will proclaim the name of the LORD before thee; and will be gracious to whom I will be gracious, and will shew mercy on whom I will shew mercy.' And he said, 'Thou canst not see my face: For there shall no man see me, and live.'

> And the LORD said, 'Behold, *there is* a place by me, and thou shalt stand upon a rock: And it shall come to pass, while my glory passeth by, that I will put thee in a clift of the rock, and will cover thee with my hand while I pass by: And I will take away mine hand, and thou shalt see my

back parts: But my face shall not be
seen.'"

Exodus 33:18 – 23

"And the LORD descended in the
cloud, and stood with him there, and
proclaimed the name of the LORD.
And the LORD passed by before him,
and proclaimed, 'The LORD, The
LORD God, merciful and gracious,
longsuffering, and abundant in
goodness and truth, keeping mercy
for thousands, forgiving iniquity and
transgression and sin, and that will by
no means clear *the guilty;* visiting the
iniquity of the fathers upon the
children, and upon the children's
children, unto the third and to the
fourth *generation.*' And Moses made
haste, and bowed his head toward
the earth, and worshipped."

Exodus 34:5 -8

In order for Moses to experience this, he had to be
so close to the Lord that God had to place His hands
over Moses' face, while He went past him. This
brought Moses into the marvelous, most awesome,
and glorious presence of Almighty God. Nowhere
has it been recorded that another man went this
close to God on the earth. This is one of the most
awesome things to have been recorded in scripture.

Anytime that anyone comes into the presence of God in such a manner, things happen. You will find that you are affected for life. Change comes. Your existence is altered for good and you are never the same person again. Moses was affected! As Moses descended from Mount Sinai, he was so transformed that the people thought that they were looking at a ghost.

> "And it came to pass, when Moses came down from Mount Sinai with the two tablets of testimony in Moses' hand, when he came down from the mount, that Moses wist not that the skin of his face shone while he talked with him."
>
> Exodus 34:29

This is not the first time that Moses was in the presence of God. Every time that he went up the mountain to meet with the Lord, he was in God's presence. The difference between this time and the other times is that God never brought him into His awesome, magnified and glorified presence. It was always at a distance. Even though there were times when it was face to face, God did not show up in His glorified state. This time He did. And Moses had a most wonderful experience with God. He was never the same again.

Every morning, Moses would go to the Tabernacle to meet with the Lord. And each morning, curious, yearning faces peered at him as he would

How To Receive Greater Anointing

pass by on his way to the Tabernacle. The people of Israel would come out of their tents, stand and watch as Moses went to meet with Jehovah.

Can you imagine how affected Moses was? Doesn't it cause you to wonder as to the degree of transformation that Moses experienced, which caused the people to want to watch him walk by? He was on his way to meet with His Maker. Why did they desire to see the man of God pass by? Perhaps they expected more change to occur. Maybe they were looking for some other great thing to happen.

Moses came down the mountain with a *greater anointing*.

"And Moses took the tabernacle, and pitched it without the camp, afar off from the camp, and called it the Tabernacle of the congregation.

And it came to pass, when Moses went out into the tabernacle, that all the people rose up, and stood every man at his tent door, and looked at

> Moses until he was gone into the tabernacle."
>
> Exodus 33:7-8

> "And it came to pass, as Moses entered into the tabernacle, that the cloudy pillar descended, and stood at the door of the tabernacle, *and the Lord talked with Moses.* And all the people saw the cloudy pillar stand at the tabernacle door: And all the people rose up and worshiped, every man in his tent door."
>
> Exodus 33:9-10

The greater anointing gave Moses access for a more intimate relationship with the Lord. Every time that he entered the Tabernacle, the Lord would meet with him in the last partition of it. This area was known as the Holy of Holies.

Imagine the relationship between this man and His God! Every morning, as Moses would enter the Tabernacle, God would descend to speak with him. Face to face, they met and conversed.

Wouldn't you love to have this kind of a relationship with the Lord? If you think that this kind of intimacy is only reserved for people like Moses, you are absolutely wrong. You can have the same kind of relationship with Jesus right now! You can visit with Him every day and hear His voice for yourself. It is not impossible!

God desires for you to have
greater anointing in your life!

And imagine the lives that would be affected
because your life was changed. All of Israel was
influenced by the great transformation of Moses.
How much influence and change do you think is
possible to those around you?

God desires for you to have greater
anointing in your life! It is not reserved for people
like Moses, preachers on television or those with
large congregations, etc. It is available to you also.
Desire it! Ask for it. God is willing and waiting to
bless you with greater anointing!

Be dissatisfied with mediocrity

Time and time again Moses went up to the Mountain
of God. He went to receive instructions from the Lord
for Israel, and to also receive the Ten
Commandments. On some of those occasions he was
there to intercede for Israel because they had
sinned against the Lord. And most of those times he

had gone up because God instructed him to. But, then came a time that Moses desired more.

God's relationship with His servant was an intimate one; they communicated constantly. They were true friends. Often the cloud of the Lord would descend at the door of the Tabernacle that Moses had set up outside their camp area. But at other times the Lord would walk in and speak face to face with Moses. He loved Moses and honoured him. And most of these times it was all about Israel. However, Moses wanted more. "Lord, show me your glory."

He was not satisfied with just instructions and visitations. He couldn't continue with just "hi and good bye." And it is not that their relationship was just "hi and good bye," it was deeper. But this man of God desired more from God. What about you?

Do you realize that God Almighty would not be angry with you if you wanted more from Him? It would bring such joy to His heart if you desired more from Him. He is not human and does not react in human ways. You have to understand that this is why He does all that He does for us. Your Father and mine, desires that you would want more intimacy with Him. It thrills Him to be close to His children. It is exactly what He wants for you to desire, more than anything else. And guess what, if you asked Him for greater intimacy; that is exactly what you would receive.

Moses said to the Lord, "I want to see your glory." Jehovah knew exactly what he meant. The Lord knew that Moses desired to see Him just as He is, face to face. Yes, Moses had spoken and seen God face to face; but not God's glorified face. He did not see Him in the heavenly form that Jesus sees Him in. He couldn't and lived.

Listen to Praise, Pray, most of all Read the Word, Wait, Fast

It is kind of like this, "Lord, you and I go back a long ways. We have been up the Mountain, down the Mountain, in the Sea and out of the Sea, all over the Desert and up the Mountain again. But, you have been keeping something from me. You say we are friends, but you do not allow me to see your glory. I want to see your glory." *Fasting, Mediate on this word in quiet moments*

"I will grant your wish. But, only the back of me you shall see. I will hide you in the Rock. I will pass by you. You are going to have an experience like none other on earth; a heavenly experience. However, you still won't be able to see my glorified face."

The man of God received what he asked for. You can too, if you would desire it with all of your heart and ask for it. You can have greater anointing!

Less talking, your opinions Godly only

Points to reconsider and ponder

- Anytime that anyone comes into the presence of God in such a manner, things happen.

- Moses came down the mountain with a *greater anointing*.

- The greater anointing gave Moses access for a more intimate relationship with the Lord.

- You can have the same kind of relationship with Jesus right now!

- God desires for you to have greater anointing in your life!

- Your Father and mine, desires that we would want more intimacy with Him. *yes*

Knowing who I am in God
Seeking to Please Him in my Spirit
Speak out "MY against Wrong

"MY
SIGNIFICANCE
IS NOT IN MY
ACCOMPLISH-
MENTS. IT IS IN
WHO I AM IN
CHRIST." yes

Chapter Eight

The Anointing

Jesus went about doing Good being a Servant to the people of God

It was time for Moses to die. His journey on the earth was over. He was one hundred and twenty years old. Yet his physical strength did not cease nor did his eyes lose their full vision. He was a remarkable example of God's keeping power.

So Moses took God's people from Egypt to the Jordan River. He took them around the Mountain for forty years. He put up with their complaints, interceded for them over and over again, and he struck the rock so that water came out for them to drink. He saw manna fall from heaven every day, and he also saw quails falling on to the earth for them to eat.

I don't want to complain

The Lord called him up to the mountain and showed him all of the Promised Land. He saw where each tribe would be and who would be on this side of Jordan and who would inherit the other side. God also told him what he had to do for the next leader who would take Israel further.

(Moses was concerned about this as all great leaders would, who love the people they lead. He was quite concerned, but the Lord said to him, "I have my leader chosen already.")

What is quite interesting is that Moses did not recognize Joshua to be the next leader. Obviously, he seemed to expect the Lord to choose someone exactly like himself. He had always thought that Israel were a great people and needed a great leader. When the Lord called him the first time from the burning bush, he didn't want to go because he was afraid that he didn't have what it would take.

(Now, he was looking for the "anointed of God." He was envisioning that it would take a man exactly like himself.) A man who had the same intimacy and knowledge of God; someone who had the same closeness with the Lord; one who had spent time with the Lord as he did, on the mountain top, in the valley, and in the Tabernacle.

He was searching for someone who would be able to raise a rod and be able to divide the red

When you are reproved Leadership @ every time it didn't make you feel as through you are what God call you be.

sea. He was expecting another great shepherd exactly like himself. And so he missed Joshua.

Joshua had become a great warrior. He led the warriors of Israel many times into battle with decisive victories. He knew how to win. The Lord gave him victories, and in his heart he was a winner. He was already groomed and prepared to go into the Promised Land, face the giants or whatever formidable force would stand before him, overcome them and destroy them. He was the man for the job.

your giftings are who you are God, no matter

Moses was looking for a shepherd with a staff. God had a shepherd with a sword!

what Man think of you.

Joshua anointed to lead

The Lord told Moses what he was to do. He would gather the people together, bring Joshua before them and place his hands upon him. God would then take a portion of His Spirit and of the gifts that he had placed in Moses, and put them on Joshua.

> "And Moses spake unto the LORD, saying, Let the LORD, the God of the spirits of all flesh, set a man over the congregation, which may go out before them, and which may go in before them, and which may lead them out, and which may bring them in; that the congregation of the LORD

Never giving other Men of God responsibilys because you don't have respect him or her in

the ministry that have been in over fifty or years but others that just come in not even knowing if they're going to stay or not.? Shameful!

be not as sheep which have no shepherd.

And the LORD said unto Moses, 'Take thee Joshua the son of Nun, a man in whom is the spirit, and lay thine hand upon him; and set him before Eleazar the priest, and before all the congregation; and give him a charge in their sight.

And thou shalt put some of thine honour upon him, that all the congregation of the children of Israel may be obedient. And he shall stand before Eleazar the priest, who shall ask counsel for him after the judgment of Urim before the LORD: at his word shall they go out, and at his word they shall come in, both he, and all the children of Israel with him, even all the congregation.'

And Moses did as the LORD commanded him: And he took Joshua, and set him before Eleazar the priest, and before all the congregation: And he laid his hands upon him, and gave him a charge, as the LORD commanded by the hand of Moses."

Numbers 27:15-23

"And Joshua the son of Nun was full of the spirit of wisdom; for Moses

Every new person gets a key

had laid his hands upon him: And the children of Israel hearkened unto him, and did as the LORD commanded Moses."

Deuteronomy 34:9

We see then that there are measures of the anointing. Moses had a greater anointing of perhaps all the prophets of the Old Testament. And that came about because of his many encounters with the Lord. But not only that, he desired more of God and asked for it over and over again.

There was the time that he told the Lord that if He didn't go with them, he wasn't going any further. Then of course there was the time when he asked the Lord to grant him the desire to see His glory.

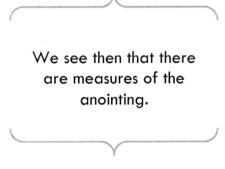

We see then that there are measures of the anointing.

Elijah and Elisha

Like Moses and Joshua, there were Elijah and Elisha. Elijah had a great anointing on his life. The power of God was mightily upon him and he did awesome miracles. Once he outran the chariot of the King. He was the one who sat by a stream and the Lord sent a raven to bring him bread and meat twice a day.

> "AND Elijah the Tishbite, *who was* of the inhabitants of Gilead, said unto Ahab, '*As* the LORD God of Israel liveth, before whom I stand, there shall not be dew nor rain these years, but according to my word.' And the word of the LORD came unto him, saying, 'Get thee hence, and turn thee eastward, and hide thyself by the brook Cherith, that *is* before Jordan. And it shall be, *that* thou shalt drink of the brook; and I have commanded the ravens to feed thee there.'
>
> So he went and did according unto the word of the LORD: For he went and dwelt by the brook Cherith, that *is* before Jordan. And the ravens brought him bread and flesh in the morning, and bread and flesh in the evening; and he drank of the brook."
>
> 1st King 17:1-6

Elisha was with Elijah like Joshua was with Moses. And Elisha desired more. When he knew that Elijah was going to be taken up to heaven in a chariot of God, he asked Elijah to give him a double portion of the anointing that was upon his life.

Elijah being a prophet understood that this was also the plan of Jehovah. And so he told Elisha that if Elisha saw him when he was being taken up, he would receive the double portion. Elijah never left Elisha's side after that. And when Elijah was taken up in the chariot of God, his mantle was caught by Elisha, and Elisha received a double portion of anointing.

He went on from there to do awesome and wonderful miracles. The first thing that he did was to divide the Jordan River. He slapped the water with the mantle of Elijah and the water separated for him to cross over.

> "And Elijah took his mantle, and wrapped *it* together, and smote the waters, and they were divided hither and thither, so that they two went over on dry ground. And it came to pass, when they were gone over, that Elijah said unto Elisha, 'Ask what I shall do for thee, before I be taken away from thee.'

And Elisha said, 'I pray thee, let a double portion of thy spirit be upon me.' And he said, 'Thou hast asked a hard thing: *Nevertheless*, if thou see me *when I am* taken from thee, it shall be so unto thee; but if not, it shall not be *so*.'

And it came to pass, as they still went on, and talked, that, behold, *there appeared* a chariot of fire, and horses of fire, and parted them both asunder; and Elijah went up by a whirlwind into heaven. And Elisha saw *it*, and he cried, 'My father, my father, the chariot of Israel, and the horsemen thereof.'

And he saw him no more: And he took hold of his own clothes, and rent them in two pieces. He took up also the mantle of Elijah that fell from him, and went back, and stood by the bank of Jordan; and he took the mantle of Elijah that fell from him, and smote the waters, and said, 'Where *is* the LORD God of Elijah?' And when he also had smitten the waters, they parted hither and thither: and Elisha went over."

2nd Kings 2:8-14

Another time a young prophet in training lost the axe head, which fell into the water. Elisha cut a piece of wood, threw it into the water, and the axe head floated.

"AND the sons of the prophets said unto Elisha, 'Behold now, the place where we dwell with thee is too strait for us. Let us go, we pray thee, unto Jordan, and take thence every man a beam, and let us make us a place there, where we may dwell' And he answered, 'Go ye.' And one said, 'Be content, I pray thee, and go with thy servants.'" And he answered, 'I will go.' So he went with them. And when they came to Jordan, they cut down wood. But as one was felling a beam, the axe head fell into the water: And he cried, and said, 'Alas, master! for it was borrowed.' And the man of God said, 'Where fell it?' And he shewed him the place. And he cut down a stick, and cast *it* in thither; and the iron did swim."

2nd Kings 6:1-6

Peter

And then we have Peter and Paul of the New Testament.

Peter was a fisherman. Jesus said to him one day, "Come follow me." He followed Jesus. He became one of Jesus' twelve disciples.

There was a time that Jesus blessed Peter and his fishing partners with a great catch of fish. The catch was so great that Peter was in shock and asked Jesus to depart from him. Peter felt like such a loser and an awful sinner. He felt terribly unworthy of Jesus' company. He was obviously under conviction of his past life. But, the Lord had plans for Peter. Jesus was going to make him a great soul winner.

> "And he entered into one of the ships, which was Simon's, and prayed him that he would thrust out a little from the land. And he sat down, and taught the people out of the ship. Now when he had left speaking, he said unto Simon, 'Launch out into the deep, and let down your nets for a draught.'
>
> And Simon answering said unto him, 'Master, we have toiled all the night, and have taken nothing: Nevertheless at thy word I will let down the net.'

And when they had this done, they inclosed a great multitude of fishes: And their net brake. And they beckoned unto *their* partners, which were in the other ship, that they should come and help them. And they came, and filled both the ships, so that they began to sink. When Simon Peter saw *it*, he fell down at Jesus' knees, saying, 'Depart from me; for I am a sinful man, O Lord.'

For he was astonished, and all that were with him, at the draught of the fishes which they had taken: And so *was* also James, and John, the sons of Zebedee, which were partners with Simon. And Jesus said unto Simon, 'Fear not; from henceforth thou shalt catch men.'"

Some of men were family but left family to follow Jesus

Luke 5:3-10

Peter and the other disciples were with Jesus for about three years. They ate with Him, slept in the same house with Him, and sailed in the fishing boats with Him. They were there when He did great miracles, like feeding thousands by multiplying loaves and fishes. They saw Him open blind eyes, and cause the deaf to hear.

They were there when people opened the roof of a house, and let their crippled friend down in front of Jesus so that He could heal the man. They were there when He touched the coffin of a young man who had died and was being taken to be buried. The young man came alive. They were also there when Jesus called out to Lazarus in the tomb, "Lazarus, come forth!"

> "And when he thus had spoken, he cried with a loud voice, 'Lazarus, come forth.' And he that was dead came forth, bound hand and foot with graveclothes: and his face was bound about with a napkin. Jesus saith unto them, 'Loose him, and let him go.'"
>
> John 11:43, 44

There came a day that the disciples were ready to be put to the task. He sent out the twelve. Then, Jesus called seventy others and sent them out two by two, to go and preach, heal the sick and cast out demons. They all came back rejoicing at how demons were subjected to them. They had seen the power of God at work through them and they were amazed. But, Jesus said, "It is because I gave you the power to do those things."

> "THEN he called his twelve disciples together, and gave them power and authority over all devils, and to cure diseases. And he sent them to preach the kingdom of God, and to heal the sick."
>
> Luke 9:1, 2

"And the seventy returned again with joy, saying, 'Lord, even the devils are subject unto us through thy name.' And he said unto them, 'I beheld Satan as lightning fall from heaven. Behold, I give unto you power to tread on serpents and scorpions, and over all the power of the enemy: and nothing shall by any means hurt you.'"

Luke 10:17-19

Pentecost

After Jesus had died and risen from the dead, He told His disciples to wait for the Holy Spirit to come. He told them that they would be empowered and be witnesses.

"THE former treatise have I made, O Theophilus, of all that Jesus began both to do and teach, until the day in which he was taken up, after that he through the Holy Ghost had given commandments unto the apostles whom he had chosen:

To whom also he shewed himself alive after his passion by many infallible proofs, being seen of them forty days, and speaking of the things pertaining to the kingdom of God: And, being assembled together with *them*, commanded them that they should not depart from Jerusalem, but wait for the promise of the Father, which, *saith he*, ye have heard of me. For John truly baptized with water; but ye shall be baptized with the Holy Ghost not many days hence."

Acts 1:1-5

"And in those days Peter stood up in the midst of the disciples, and said, (the number of names together were about an hundred and twenty,)...

'Men and brethren, this scripture must needs have been fulfilled, which the Holy Ghost...spake...'"

Acts 1:15-16a

When the day of Pentecost came, there were about one hundred and twenty of them in one place, waiting for the Holy Spirit to descend. With a mighty rushing wind, He fell upon all of them! The room was filled with God's presence. They all spoke in other tongues as the Holy Spirit spoke through them. They received greater anointing.

"AND when the day of Pentecost was fully come, they were all with one accord in one place. And suddenly there came a sound from heaven as of a rushing mighty wind, and it filled all the house where they were sitting. And there appeared unto them cloven tongues like as of fire, and it sat upon each of them. And they were all filled with the Holy Ghost, and began to speak with other tongues, as the Spirit gave them utterance."

Acts 2:1-4

It was early in the morning. When they came out of the place that they were in, people thought that they were all drunk. But, Peter stood up and preached perhaps the message of his life. Three thousand came to Christ and joined the disciples. The gospel then spread like fire throughout the known world.

"And they were all amazed, and were in doubt, saying one to another, 'What meaneth this?' Others mocking said, 'These men are full of new wine.'"

Acts 2:12, 13

"But Peter, standing up with the eleven, lifted up his voice, and said unto them..."

"Then Peter said unto them, 'Repent, and be baptized every one of you in the name of Jesus Christ for the remission of sins, and ye shall receive the gift of the Holy Ghost. For the promise is unto you, and to your children, and to all that are afar off, *even* as many as the Lord our God shall call.' And with many other words did he testify and exhort, saying, 'Save yourselves from this untoward generation.' Then they that gladly received his word were baptized: And the same day there were added *unto* *them* about three thousand souls."

Acts 2:14, 38-41

Paul Formerly Called Saul at natural Birth, but after spiritual Birth on the

I must not forget to tell you about Paul. Paul's first name was Saul. And He was a champion of the cause of those who were against Christianity. He took many Christians to prison and saw many killed for what he thought was just cause. But God had a plan for him. And one day as he was on his way to capture many more Christians to drag them off to prison or to kill them, the Lord met him.

"AND Saul, yet breathing out threatenings and slaughter against the disciples of the Lord, went unto the high priest, and desired of him letters to Damascus to the way to kill More of God's Saints in the City of Damascus synagogues, that if he found any of this way, whether they were men or women, he might bring them bound unto Jerusalem. And as he journeyed, he came near Damascus: And suddenly there shined round about him a light from heaven:

And he fell to the earth, and heard a voice saying unto him, 'Saul, Saul, why persecutest thou me?' And he said, 'Who art thou, Lord?' And the Lord said, 'I am Jesus whom thou persecutest: *it is* hard for thee to kick against the pricks.' And he trembling and astonished said, 'Lord, what wilt thou have me to do?'

And the Lord *said* unto him, 'Arise, and go into the city, and it shall be told thee what thou must do.' And the men which journeyed with him stood speechless, hearing a voice, but seeing no man. And Saul arose from the earth; and when his eyes were opened, he saw no man: But they led him by the hand, and brought *him* into Damascus."

Acts 9:1-8

"And he was three days without sight, and neither did eat nor drink. And there was a certain disciple at Damascus, named Ananias; and to him said the Lord in a vision, 'Ananias.' And he said, 'Behold, I *am here*, Lord.' And the Lord *said* unto him, 'Arise, and go into the street which is called Straight, and inquire in the house of Judas for *one* called Saul, of Tarsus: For, behold, he prayeth, and hath seen in a vision a man named Ananias coming in, and putting *his* hand on him, that he might receive his sight.'

God's Word is Sure & True Believe It and do it as he speaks it to you

Then Ananias answered, 'Lord, I have heard by many of this man, how much evil he hath done to thy saints at Jerusalem: And here he hath authority from the chief priests to bind all that call on thy name.'

But the Lord said unto him, 'Go thy way: for he is a chosen vessel unto me, to bear my name before the Gentiles, and kings, and the children of Israel: For I will shew him how great things he must suffer for my name's sake.' And Ananias went his way, and entered into the house; and putting his hands on him said, 'Brother Saul, the Lord, *even* Jesus, that appeared unto thee in the way as thou camest, hath sent me, that thou mightest receive thy sight, and be *filled with the Holy Ghost*' And immediately there fell from his eyes as it had been scales: And he received sight forthwith, and arose, and was baptized."

Acts 9:9-18

Called by God, he was now headed in an opposite direction and on the road to glorify Jesus.

Later, as Paul went on his journey preaching and working for Jesus, he encountered some men who were baptized in water. But they did not know that there was such a thing as the baptism of the Holy Spirit. Paul laid his hands on them and prayed for them, and they received the baptism of the Holy Spirit.

"AND it came to pass, that, while Apollos was at Corinth, Paul having passed through the upper coasts came to Ephesus: And finding certain disciples, He said unto them, 'Have ye received the Holy Ghost since ye believed?' And they said unto him, 'We have not so much as heard whether there be any Holy Ghost.' And he said unto them, 'Unto what then were ye baptized?' And they said, 'Unto John's baptism'.

Then said Paul, 'John verily baptized with the baptism of repentance, saying unto the people, that they should believe on him which should come after him, that is, on Christ Jesus.' When they heard *this*, they were baptized in the name of the Lord Jesus. And when Paul had laid *his* hands upon them, *the Holy Ghost came on them*; and they spake with tongues, and prophesied. And all the men were about twelve."

Acts 19:1-7

Timothy

Some people try to smother you gifting by keeping setting down in Church, that you have a God to satisfy not man

Timothy was a Christian who followed Paul. As a matter of fact Paul calls him his son. Paul reminded him to stir up the gift within him that was given to him by the laying on of hands. This is most likely the baptism of the Holy Spirit and Paul was encouraging him to not quench the Spirit, but to stir up the anointing that was in him.

"To Timothy, *my* dearly beloved son: Grace, mercy, *and* peace, from God the Father and Christ Jesus our Lord."

2nd Timothy 1:2

"Wherefore I put thee in remembrance that thou stir up the gift of God, which is in thee by the putting on of my hands. For God hath not given us the spirit of fear; but of power, and of love, and of a sound mind."

Sure you are Right Brother

Some times you have to go away from home Church to perfect your gift no matter others think of you

2nd Timothy 1:6, 7

All these examples demonstrate to us that not only is there an anointing, but that there is greater anointing. Every one of these men were transformed and empowered by the anointing. And there were those who passed it on to others by the laying on of their hands.

So your anointing becomes greater don't get Holys than Thou Attude

Holy Spirit and anointing

What is the connection between the Holy Spirit and the anointing?

In the Old Testament, Priests and Kings were anointed with oil as they were placed into their position as Priest or King. The anointing oil is a representation of the Holy Spirit. It demonstrates the fact that this is a chosen of God and the office is holy, consecrated and separated unto God. God was placing His Spirit upon a man, for a holy office and function. The anointed was to fulfill his role in a holy and reverent manner. This was a thing unto God. It was not to be taken lightly or as an ordinary matter.

When Saul was chosen to be King, Samuel poured oil on him and the Spirit of God came upon him. And when he was in the company of the prophets, he prophesied.

The anointing oil is a representation of the Holy Spirit.

"THEN Samuel took a vial of oil, and poured *it* upon his head, and kissed him, and said, '*Is it* not because the LORD hath anointed thee *to be* captain over his inheritance? When thou art departed from me today, then thou shalt find two men by Rachel's sepulchre in the border of Benjamin at Zelzah; and they will say unto thee, The asses which thou wentest to seek are found: and, lo, thy father hath left the care of the asses, and sorroweth for you, saying, What shall I do for my son?

Then shalt thou go on forward from thence, and thou shalt come to the plain of Tabor, and there shall meet thee three men going up to God to Beth-el, one carrying three kids, and another carrying three loaves of bread, and another carrying a bottle of wine: And they will salute thee, and give thee two *loaves* of bread; which thou shalt receive of their hands.

After that thou shalt come to the hill of God, where *is* the garrison of the Philistines: and it shall come to pass, when thou art come thither to the city, that thou shalt meet a company of prophets coming down from the high place with a psaltery, and a tabret, and a pipe, and a harp, before them; and they shall prophesy: *And the Spirit of the LORD will come upon thee*, and thou shalt prophesy with them, and shalt be turned into another man. And let it be, when these signs are come unto thee, *that* thou do as occasion serve thee; for God *is* with thee.'"

1Samuel 10: 1-7

"And it was *so*, that when he had turned his back to go from Samuel, God gave him another heart: And all those signs came to pass that day. And when they came thither to the

> hill, behold, a company of prophets met him; and the Spirit of God came upon him, and he prophesied among them.
>
> And it came to pass, when all that knew him beforetime saw that, behold, he prophesied among the prophets, then the people said one to another, 'What *is* this *that* is come unto the son of Kish? *Is* Saul also among the prophets?'"
>
> 1st Samuel 10:9-11

You will notice that after Samuel anointed Saul to be King, he pointed out to him a number of things that would happen. One of those things was that he would meet a group of prophets. They would be worshipping and they would prophesy, and the Spirit of God would come upon Saul and he too would prophesy.

Saul could have prophesied right there in front of Samuel. But that is not how the Lord wanted it. Saul was from a small unknown family. To make him known and in a great way, this is how God chose to have it happen. After this, Saul was known throughout the land as one who prophesied.

> "And Saul answered and said, '*Am* not I a Benjamite, of the smallest of the tribes of Israel? And my family the least of all the families of the

tribe of Benjamin?   Wherefore then speakest thou so to me?

1st Samuel 9:21

Aaron also had oil poured upon him when he was ordained to be a priest of God.

> "And thou shalt take the garments, and put upon Aaron the coat, and the robe of the ephod, and the ephod, and the breastplate, and gird him with the curious girdle of the ephod: And thou shalt put the mitre upon his head, and put the holy crown upon the mitre. Then shalt thou take the anointing oil, and pour *it* upon his head, and anoint him."
>
> Exodus 29: 5-7

Jesus said that He was going to send the Holy Spirit after He was gone back to Heaven. He said that Holy Spirit would comfort us, guide us and teach us. The Holy Spirit is the Spirit of truth. When someone receives Jesus Christ as Lord and Saviour, the Holy Spirit comes to reside in that person's spirit.

> "But when the Comforter is come, whom I will send unto you from the Father, *even* the Spirit of truth, which proceedeth from the Father, he shall testify of me:"
>
> John 15:26

"Nevertheless I tell you the truth; it is expedient for you that I go away: For if I go not away, the Comforter will not come unto you; but if I depart, I will send him unto you. Howbeit when he, the Spirit of truth, is come, he will guide you into all truth: For he shall not speak of himself; but whatsoever he shall hear, *that* shall he speak: And he will shew you things to come."

John 16:7, 13

Jesus said that He would not leave us comfortless, He would come to us. He came by the Holy Spirit. The Holy Spirit is the Spirit of God and the Spirit of Christ. Therefore, Jesus Christ resides in the believer by the Holy Spirit.

"If ye love me, keep my commandments. And I will pray the Father, and he shall give you another Comforter, that he may abide with you for ever; *even* the Spirit of truth; whom the world cannot receive, because it seeth him not, neither knoweth him: But ye know him; for he dwelleth with you, and shall be in you. I will not leave you comfortless: I will come to you."

John 14:15-18

The Holy Spirit is also called "The Anointing." And this is the connection of the Holy Spirit and anointing.

> "But the anointing which ye have received of him abideth in you, and ye need not that any man teach you: But as the same anointing teacheth you of all things, and is truth, and is no lie, and even as it hath taught you, ye shall abide in him."
>
> 1st John 2:27

Greater anointing is coming and everyone can receive it. As a matter of fact, God is no respecter of persons and whatever He has for us is for all of us to share.

In the book of Acts we see the Lord pouring out His Spirit on those who were waiting. Jesus had told His disciples to wait for the outpouring of God's Spirit.

There were about five hundred followers of Jesus altogether, but only about one hundred and twenty received the Holy Spirit baptism on the day of Pentecost. What about the others? Where were they? How come they didn't wait with the one hundred and twenty? There is nothing mentioned about them, whether they also received the baptism of the Holy Spirit.

> "For I delivered unto you first of all that which I also received, how that

Christ died for our sins according to the scriptures; And that he was buried, and that he rose again the third day according to the scriptures: And that he was seen of Cephas, then of the twelve:

After that, he was seen of *above five hundred brethren* at once; of whom the greater part remain unto this present, but some are fallen asleep."

1st Corinthians 15: 3-7

"*The Lord is not slack concerning His promise,* as some men count slackness; but is longsuffering to us-ward, not willing that *any* should perish, but that all should come to repentance."

2nd Peter 3:9"

It is crucial for us to be ready! The Lord has promised, and what He promises, He will make sure that it comes to pass. Get ready!

Points to reconsider and ponder

- God would then take a portion of His Spirit and gifts that he had placed in Moses, and put them on Joshua.

- We see then that there are measures of the anointing.

- Moses had a greater anointing of perhaps all the prophets of the Old Testament. And that came about because of his many encounters with the Lord.

- All these examples demonstrate to us that not only is there an anointing, but that there is greater anointing.

- The anointing oil is a representation of the Holy Spirit.

- The Holy Spirit is also called "The Anointing."

- The Lord has promised, and what He promises, He will make sure that it comes to pass.

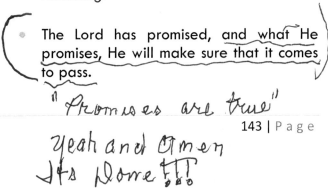

"Promises are true"

Yeah and Amen
Its Done!!!

"STOP LIVING IN THE OASIS OF 'WHAT IFS' AND START LIVING IN THE GARDEN OF 'WHAT COULD BE.'"

Chapter Nine

All Things Are Ready

How can you tell when things are ready?

If you are a chef, you know that there is only so long that you can have that chicken in the oven. Just a little too much over the limit and it will be burnt. You have the telltale aroma to know when it is finished. And the nice sugar brown appearance tells you it is time to remove it from the oven.

If you are a gardener, you understand that some plants grow better in the shade while others love the sun. And you know how much water is sufficient. Before picking the fruits, you recognize the time to pick them. You know that they will ripen and fall off if you do not pick them on time. The birds definitely will get them if you do not!

There are revealing signs as well all around us which say to us, "All things are ready." Do you see the signs? Are you looking for them?

> "And Jesus answered and spake unto them again by parables, and said, "The kingdom of heaven is like unto a certain King, which made a marriage for his son, and sent forth his servants to call them that were bidden to the wedding: And they would not come.
>
> Again, he sent forth other servants, saying, 'Tell them which are bidden, behold I have prepared my dinner: My oxen and my fatlings are killed and all things are ready: come unto the marriage.'
> But they made light of it, and went their ways, one to his farm, another to his merchandise. And the remnant took his servants, and entreated them spitefully, and slew them.
>
> But when the king heard thereof, he was wroth: And he sent forth his armies, and destroyed those murderers and burned up their city.
> Then saith he to his servants, 'The wedding is ready, but they that were bidden were not worthy. Go ye therefore into the highways, and as

many as ye shall find, bid to the marriage.'

So those servants went out into the highways, and gathered together all as many as they found, both bad and good: And the wedding was furnished with guests. And when the king came in to see the guests, he saw there a man which had not on a wedding garment: And he saith unto him, 'Friend, how camest thou in hither not having a wedding garment?' And he was speechless.

Then said the king to the servants, 'Bind him hand and foot, and take him away, and cast him into outer darkness. There shall be weeping and gnashing of teeth. For many are called but few are chosen.'"
Matthew 22: 1-14

God's servants proclaimed good news for four thousand years. Prophets prophesied to the nation, crying "repent, repent; serve God." Many were ridiculed, beaten and killed. Many were mocked, laughed at and cast out. Some were listened to and obeyed while others were ignored and rejected.

As the hour drew closer, the Lord sent others to proclaim that the time had come. All things were ready. Eventually the Son came. Finally, the One who was proclaimed by the prophets had arrived. He was here: Jesus of Nazareth, Messiah, Christ! But, the Jewish people did not recognize Him. They refused Him.

For three and a half years Jesus preached the good news to them, healed their sick and raised their dead. Yet, they did not accept Him. The entire nation of Israel was called, but only a few were chosen. The whole nation of Israel was called, but only a hand full received the Messiah. Only a small number believed and accepted Christ. They were chosen.

Many are called, but few are chosen. Only those who believe are chosen.

"And they said, 'Believe on the Lord Jesus Christ, and thou <u>shalt</u> be saved, and thy house.'"
Acts 16:30-31

Those who believe are chosen, because salvation is of faith in Jesus Christ and in none other.

It is not that God comes along and goes, "This egg is mine, that one is yours." He does not say, "You are mine and you are not." He doesn't do that. God's desire is that all be saved. Jesus died for the entire world not for one or two. And all who believe shall be saved.

We don't know: God has Saved

> There are revealing signs as well all around us which say to us, "All things are ready."

Good News Preached

Therefore, for another two thousand years God again sent His servants. They preached the good news, healed the sick and raised the dead. They proclaimed the same gospel, "The Kingdom of God is at hand. It is here; receive it. Christ is coming again." They too were rejected and killed. They too were despised and refused.

For four thousand years the preachers preached and the people refused to hear. And when Messiah arrived, John the Baptist cried, "He is here. Go out to meet Him. Here is the Christ, the Lamb of God."

Those who heard Him and believed were saved. But soon, John too was killed. The farmers went to their farms, and the merchants to their shops. The priest went to the temple and continued his rituals. The religious ones went about doing religious things. And the sinner continued to sin. They did not take the day or the hour seriously. They were not afraid, nor had they urgency in their spirits. They went about doing their own thing and living life as if tomorrow was guaranteed forever. Everyone went their separate ways and did his own thing.

The tax collector went to his tax collecting, the Judge to his courthouse, and the Priest to his Priesthood. The housewife went to attend to her house and her children, the religious ones went to the temple. Shepherds went to attend their flocks while merchants went to merchandise their goods.

Messiah came, and soon, He was gone. They missed Him!

Not too long after, the armies came and destroyed those people and their city. Messiah had said to his servants, "Go into the highways and invite everyone to the wedding."

The door is now open. The gentiles can now enter in. Good and bad are invited. The religious and sinner are called. Everyone and anyone can now have a place at the table. They will be washed, sanctified, and given wedding garments, robes of righteousness. Hallelujah! All a person need do is to answer the call.

For two thousand years it was proclaimed. And for two thousand years many have heard and believed and are saved. But many others took the news lightly, did not choose Jesus, and are burning in hell today!

Many chose to do like the Jews of old. They were busy. They did their own thing. They went to their farms and to their stores. They went to their courthouses, their temples, and their homes. They took things lightly. They ignored the trumpet call and they paid the price.

Do not take things lightly! Heed the call! All things are ready. The hour is now, and the time is at hand. The Lord said to me, "There is a greater anointing coming to set the church in order for the coming of the Lord."

The Lord said it and so it will be! Be wise in this hour. Heed the call! Make the crooked ways straight. Strengthen the feeble knees. Lift up the hands that hang down.

> *"And whosoever shall exalt himself shall be abased; and he that shall humble himself shall be exalted."*
> Matthew 23: 12

Do not be high minded in this hour. Do not be wise in your own eyes. Humble yourself, and you will be exalted. Many are called but few are chosen. Live your life as if Jesus Christ might come today, to take

His Body - the Church - to be with Him. Watch and pray as the Bible says. You never know when the Lord will come.

Seek after the Lord. Ask Him to give you greater anointing. He has said that He is sending it. Therefore hesitate not! Go after it.

Joshua told Israel that when they saw the Arc of the covenant going into the Jordan River, they were to go after it. In the Arc of the covenant was the presence of God! Dear child of God, go after the presence of God. Ask the Lord for greater anointing. He will pour His Spirit upon you! He will give you greater anointing. Ask Him!

Finally brethren, let me encourage you to read this book over again. It is fast reading and there are some things that I am sure that you quickly by-passed. When you read again, this time a little slower, you are going to find those nuggets. God bless you!